# The Friendship Book

**A THOUGHT FOR EACH DAY** | **2017**

# The Friendship Book

SEEK a fresh goal every day,
Look on all things new,
Show a smile along the way,
Let happiness shine through.

Don't give up if plans first fail,
Make another start.
Keep a trust, if hope is frail,
And faith within the heart.

Set aside a time to care,
And then you'll find it's true,
A kindness passed around to share
Will be returned to you.

– Elizabeth Gozney.

# January

EVERY first of January, so it says in the 1862 Book of Days, is at once a resting place for thought and meditations, and a starting point for fresh exertion in the performance of our journey.

The Book of Days then goes on, rather cheekily, to suggest that, "The man who does not at least propose to himself to be better this year than he was last, must either be very good or very bad indeed."

Well, I think most of us probably fall somewhere in the middle of that assessment; not too bad – but not as good as we might be.

Resolutions are all very well – and often all very temporary – but if we try to be better this year than we were last year, and then do the same next year, then step by step, year by year, we shall edge ever closer to being "very good indeed".

As we commit to such improvements, we become very aware of the limitations of our will-power. But there is always help on hand.

Drawing on the Good Lord's strength and support, may we all be new and better creations in His service, in this year of 2017 and beyond.

## Monday — January 2

I DO like those jokes about the difference between optimists and pessimists. This one seems appropriate for this time of year.

"An optimist stays up all night to see the New Year arrive. A pessimist stays up all night to make sure the old year leaves." Which did you do?

How about being neither one of those, but being the kind of person that leaves one year in good repair and looks forward to making the next one even better?

## Tuesday — January 3

*IT sometimes seems we travel blind,*
*Weighed down with fear and care,*
*We stumble on a lonely path*
*En route to who knows where.*

*Yet if we choose, the lamp of hope*
*Can make the dark less black,*
*And faith, that good and steadfast guide*
*Can keep us safe on track.*

*So look around, you'll surely see*
*That others march beside,*
*This path is where we're meant to be.*
*Walk tall, and walk with pride.*

– Margaret Ingall.

## Wednesday — January 4

J.M. BARRIE, the author of "Peter Pan" and "A Window In Thrums", once said, "The life of every man is a diary in which they mean to write one story but write another; and the humblest hour is when you compare the volume as it is with what you vowed to make it."

As a writer of some experience he would know that stories don't always end the way the author imagined they would.

An author once told me of repeatedly rewriting a fight scene because the wrong character kept winning!

Many of us will be starting new diaries with the New Year. Let us aim not only to fill them, but to fill their days with tales of love shared and kindnesses offered.

We might well, as Mr Barrie pointed out, fall short, but in our "humblest hour" we will see that our so-called-failures still consist of love and kindness – and that's never a bad story to write.

In the "struggle" to fill that diary let us make sure our better character wins.

Cold as ice!

## Thursday — January 5

THE entrance to the Cathedral of the Isles on Millport is at the back and to one side. So when you walk in you don't see the whole church and you are slightly hidden from anyone further inside.

Stepping in with the Lady of the House, I announced us with a hearty, "Hello!"

I saw the lady dusting down the pews stop, step into the aisle, take a few steps towards the altar, and say, "Hello?" in return.

I introduced us, and we all got chatting. She gave us the tour, interspersing stories about the cathedral with memories of her own life. We had tea together and she told us we would be welcome back any time. Then she returned to her dust-cloth devotions.

Walking away from the cathedral some time later, I commented, "Well, we really got to know a lot about her!"

"We got to know the most important thing," the Lady of the House informed me. "That when alone in the church and she heard a voice saying hello, she automatically assumed it was God talking."

We should all have such simple, everyday, but profound faith!

## Friday — January 6

THE Feast of Epiphany celebrates the visit to the infant Jesus by the Magi. But who were the Magi? We assume there were three of them – but we don't know. We call them kings – but they might not have been.

We know they came from the East, they travelled a long way, paid their respects to the Lord. Their traditions weren't Christian but they have since become a major part of our Christmas celebrations.

When we think of them we might consider others who live different lives in different lands from ours. If we have a love of God in common then everything else ought to be secondary. Indeed, we might extend that courtesy to others in our own land.

Let's accept the gifts they have to give and offer ours in return, in appreciation of the Magi and the One they travelled so far to worship.

**P**ARTLY work and partly play," Robert Herrick wrote in 1648, "ye must on St Distaff's Day."

The day after Twelfth Night (with all the celebrations over Christmas and New Year) was traditionally a much-needed transitional day.

Half the day might be spent at work, in the times when most work was agricultural and couldn't be abandoned entirely, but there would be an early finish and the rest of the day would almost certainly be spent resting and recovering.

Hopefully we will all have had a good time over the festive period, but won't have celebrated so much that we are still recovering on January 7!

And, thankfully, our labours will not have been as hard as those of the farming folk from times gone by.

Life is made up of work and play. Both are very important and we wouldn't appreciate either one of them half so much without the other.

Let's try to have a healthy mix of both in the year ahead.

## Sunday — January 8

**W**E recently heard this little story and found it extremely heartwarming.

The human eye is so wonderfully formed that if someone was standing on top of a mountain on a clear night with an unobstructed view they could see the light of a candle thirty miles away. Isn't that amazing?

Of course we don't live on mountain tops and our views are rarely unobstructed. There can be myriad physical and emotional barriers between us and the people out there who need to see our light.

So if we don't want always to be climbing mountains, we might need to shine brighter when we can!

*Neither do people light a lamp and put it under a bowl. Instead they put it on its stand, and it gives light to everyone in the house.* Matthew 5:15-16.

## Monday — January 9

I WAS very interested to read the Nightingale Pledge recently. It is based on the Hippocratic Oath and named after the inspirational nurse, Florence Nightingale.

It contains promises about best practice, maintaining confidentiality, never knowingly doing harm and working as part of the medical team for the greater good of the patient. The 1935 version of it ends with the line, "I will dedicate myself to devoted service for human welfare."

Pledges are only as wonderful as the intention in the heart of the person making them, but wouldn't it be wonderful if we all had our own version, pledging to do whatever we can in "devoted service for human welfare"?

## Tuesday — January 10

DOESN'T it seem like every time you try to do something new there are "old hands" telling you it's a waste of time?

It's just part of the human condition, I'm afraid, and always has been. In 1592, a young actor who had ambitions to be a writer was called an "upstart crow" by members of the writing fraternity. They gathered together to put an embargo on his work and make sure he never became a threat to their livelihood.

He didn't let it stop him and neither should we. Refusing to be told he couldn't or shouldn't do something he felt strongly about enabled William Shakespeare to share his gift with the whole world.

## Wednesday — January 11

THE poet Norman MacCaig once declared, "I am a happy man and most of my poems are about praising things."

A wonderful position to be in, and one, I might suggest, that we can all achieve. You see, happiness naturally leads to praise. But praise, just as naturally, leads to happiness.

Try living your life as a thank you, and see if it doesn't lead to a life worth saying thank you for!

Winter friend.

## Thursday — January 12

HAVE you ever said something you later regretted? I'm guessing we all have in the heat of the moment, responding wrongly to something misunderstood. The psychologist and concentration camp survivor Viktor Frankl put it into words.

"Between stimulus and response," he wrote, "there is a space. In that space is our power to choose our response. In our response lies our growth and our freedom."

Take that moment – that space – to choose kindly, and be free from having to say "I didn't really mean it" ever again.

## Friday — January 13

I HAVE a friend who logs into his laptop by smiling at the screen. The camera recognises his face – how sci-fi is that? Despite all advancements in technology, some things remain uniquely ours.

I was reminded of it recently when a friend pointed out that God gave us each an individual fingerprint so we can each make an individual impression on life. Let's make sure it's a good one!

## Saturday — January 14

HAVE you ever entwined your fingers with someone else's? An anonymous wit said, "There are spaces between our fingers so another person's fingers can fill them in."

It is true that our best relationships are usually complementary ones, where the patience of one makes up for the haste of the other, for example.

Two together become more wonderful than they could ever hope to be apart. When relationships are right we make each other better.

Perhaps that's what the poet Kahlil Gibran meant when he wrote, "Let there be spaces in your togetherness, and let the winds of the heavens dance between you."

The spaces are important. If we fill them with love it will seem like heaven.

## Sunday — January 15

"THERE is scarcely any earthly object," Robert Burns wrote, "gives me more – I do not know if I should call it pleasure – but something which exalts me – than to walk in the sheltered side of a wood in a cloudy winter day, and hear the stormy wind howling among the trees and raving over the plain. It is my best season for devotion."

We never feel God's protection – as Burns did through the shelter of the wood – as much as when the storm rages. Those times are good reminders of that, although we ought to remember them always and make every season our best for devotion.

## Monday — January 16

HANDSEL MONDAY is a near-forgotten tradition. On this day people would give gifts to servants, children or poorer members of the community. In times of hardship a few coins would have been a real blessing. "Handse" or "Hansel" means something given directly from my hand to yours.

The gifts were said to symbolise prosperity in the year ahead for the recipients. Perhaps the money and the contact actually helped bring about that prosperity, but I would suggest that the greatest benefits such gifts bring go to those who bestow them!

## Tuesday — January 17

WHAT'S the most important title someone can have? And how do you get it?

Well, you have to be born into royalty to be a king or a queen. Someone who is awarded a knighthood or made a dame has probably worked for a worthwhile cause. No-one would doubt the title of President of the United States is a prestigious one, but when he was elected George Washington had something else in mind.

"I hope," he said, "that I shall possess firmness and virtue enough to maintain what I consider the most enviable of all titles, the character of an honest man."

It's another title that doesn't come easily, but it is one that is well worth working for.

## Wednesday — January 18

SOME time ago Mark Twain, author of "The Adventures Of Tom Sawyer" and "The Adventures Of Huckleberry Finn", provided the world with his personal recipe for an ideal life. It was, "Good friends, good books, and a sleepy conscience."

I would only add that if you have lived the kind of life where your conscience can justifiably take regular naps, then you are probably already living something close to an ideal life.

Good friends and good books will simply be the icing on the cake.

## Thursday — January 19

DO you remember the old Edison Lighthouse song "Love Grows (Where My Rosemary Goes)"? It was a hit quite a while ago – 1970, if you can believe that!

Mathilde Blind, the German-born British poet, was born in 1841, but she wrote along similar lines.

"Ah, life grows lovely where you are," is one of her more memorable lines.

Do you have someone like that in your life? Or will you be that person for someone else today?

## Friday — January 20

IN a world where weapons of war are growing ever more sophisticated, I'd like to offer this opinion from the inspirational writer Augustine (Og) Mandino on the ultimate weapon.

"I will make love my greatest weapon and none on whom I call can defend against its force. . . Yet my love will melt all hearts liken to the sun whose rays soften the coldest clay."

Of course, love doesn't only have to be used in times of conflict, like when President Lincoln promised to destroy his enemies by making them his friends. Hearts can also be melted in times of peace and tranquillity.

## Saturday — January 21

*ONCE, beside some tumbling falls*
*A thrilling sight held me enthralled.*
*Flashes of silver drew my eye,*
*As salmon leapt towards the sky.*
*Battling the torrential force*
*The fish strove on to keep their course.*
*They did not fail to persevere*
*Although their route was so unclear.*
*Now, when I struggle to see my way*
*I think of what I learned that day.*
*The salmon leapt, and seemed to fly.*
*The salmon leapt, and so can I.*

– Flo Jones.

## Sunday — January 22

THE Spanish have a tradition that sunshine on this day, St Vincent's Day, predicts bumper harvests in the year ahead. They have a rhyme that concludes, "For 'tis a token, bright and clear, of prosperous weather all the year."

That would be nice. But I rather favour the words of an old English shepherd who is reputed to have said, "If the Lord chooses to send rain, why then, rain's my choice, too!"

And trust that the Lord sends the right amount of each.

## Monday — January 23

WE all have our insecurities and doubts, don't we? Those little voices certainly don't represent the best of us and should probably be put firmly in their place.

Even Vincent van Gogh was prone to them. He said, "If you hear a voice within you say, 'You cannot paint', then by all means paint – and the voice will be silenced!"

So, that thing you have been putting off because you didn't think you could do it – do it. By all means do it!

## Tuesday — January 24

I HAD passed this pond often and noticed that its residents never really got on. But a layer of snow lay around the banks that day and the pond was gradually freezing from the outer edges in. When I threw some bread, the swans, ducks and small birds all paddled around each other, catching whatever came in range.

Walking away, I reflected that a pond of birds was an unlikely metaphor for humanity, but it warmed my heart just thinking that while we, too, will squabble and squawk in times of plenty, in times of need we also work together and share what we have.

As the poet Longfellow said, "Then come the wild weather – come sleet or come snow, we will stand by each other, however it blow."

## Wednesday — January 25

ON the day that celebrates Scotland's national poet I remember that Alfred, Lord Tennyson, thought Robert Burns's songs had "the light and radiance of a dewdrop" but dismissed his serious poetry. Meanwhile, Wordsworth thought the songs best forgotten but praised him as having "brought poetry back to nature."

Burns, thankfully, carried on doing what he did, regardless of who thought what, being true to himself and his work. To paraphrase him, he was who he was – as should we all be – "for a' that."

## Thursday — January 26

MARGERITE GARDINER, who was Countess of Blessington in the early 19th century, met many famous people on her travels. She once said, "Mountains appear more lofty the nearer they are approached, but great men resemble them not in this particular."

In other words, the best of the great men were, once you got to know them, not lofty at all but quite down to earth.

It's one thing to stand above others in your supposed greatness, but mountain peaks must get very lonely up there in the clouds while life and love go on in the foothills and valleys. Be great, by all means – but in an approachable, useful, sort of way.

## Friday — January 27

*I 'LL cherish the here and now,*
*Not worry way ahead,*
*But delight in each new moment*
*Of this day instead.*
*I won't scan the far horizon*
*Searching for the rain,*
*But enjoy the present sunny skies,*
*Then I will surely gain*
*Strength from being happy,*
*Joy from being glad,*
*To cheer me like a sunbeam*
*If I feel down or sad.*
*I'll leave to God the future,*
*Trust Him all the way,*
*And thank Him for each precious hour*
*He's given me this day!*

– Marian Cleworth.

## Saturday — January 28

LOOK around if you visit Amsterdam and you might spot a repair café. You may well ask – as I had to – what a repair café is.

The cafés are also workshops. If you have a wobbly chair, damaged crockery, torn and worn clothing, the experts there will show you how to give them a second lease of life – over coffee and a cake.

As well as a contented tummy, you take away with you the knowledge of the repair, which you can then pass on to others. With more things being repaired instead of replaced, the demand for resources (so the theory goes) will be reduced and the dear old earth will get a bit of a rest. A tea break, some might say.

A wonderful idea, but it occurred to me there was another possible interpretation of the name. Any time we share a cuppa and a listening ear with someone, every time we leave someone feeling better for having spent time together, we are, each of us, running our very own repair café.

I'll raise a cup of tea (and a chocolate biscuit) to that!

## Sunday — January 29

SOMETIMES it helps to see our situation through the eyes of an outsider – even if that outsider is a horse!

In her classic novel "Black Beauty", Anna Sewell wrote, "There is no religion without love, and people may talk as much as they like about religion, but if it does not teach them to be good and kind to man and beast it is all a sham."

*Religion that God our Father accepts as pure and faultless is this: to look after orphans and widows in their distress and to keep oneself from being polluted by the world.* James 1:27.

## Monday — January 30

ON this day in 1939 President Franklin D. Roosevelt decided to hold a Birthday Ball, although, as a sufferer of childhood polio, he couldn't dance. The ball was a fund-raiser to make sure other children, in the future, could.

The National Foundation For Infantile Paralysis eventually came into being, funded in large part by donations of ten cent pieces from mothers all across America. Many of those mothers would have struggled to spare a dime, but millions of them thought it a cause worth helping – a dime at a time.

We all have some little thing we can do to make a difference for the better. If the cause is a good one others will add their "dime" to yours and the difference made will be worth dancing about.

## Tuesday — January 31

I'D say it's a poor sort of soul who expects to be paid for living a good life. But the poet Ella Wheeler Wilcox suggested we might be rewarded for our efforts.

She wrote:   *If one poor burdened toiler o'er life's road,*
*Who meets us by the way,*
*Goes on less conscious of his galling load,*
*Then life, indeed, does pay.*

I'd work (and live) for those wages, wouldn't you?

Time ticks on.

# February

A N old folk tradition describes February as a rosy-cheeked country maid, pulling her shawl tight around her, wiping her hair from her face and walking carefully over the frozen snow – but all the while looking out for the buds on the hedgerows, delighting in the songs of the birds, and appreciating the blossom on the blackthorn. In other words, finding beauty even in the bleakest of days.

She would have got on well with the romantic poet William Cullen Bryant who wrote, "The February sunshine steeps your boughs and tints the buds and swells the leaves within."

Aware of the difficulties of the day but not cowed by them, looking forward to better and certain she won't be disappointed, Miss February sounds like a fine example for the rest of us to follow!

O N the approach to Philip's farm stands an old oak. As we drove around it I wondered out loud why it hadn't been felled like the others when Philip's forebears had been clearing the land. It looked at least as old as his farmhouse.

He didn't know about that particular tree but he recalled an old tradition that said farmers used to leave at least one tree standing so they and their workers could rest in its shade as they took their lunch break on sunny days.

So, clearing the trees helped man – but having a tree there also helped. And, of course, while we had that one tree left we always had the potential for a new forest. Careful husbandry worked to the benefit of both the trees and the people.

Thankfully, we seem to be learning that, in parts of the world anyway.

May we value what we have while we still have it and plant enough trees so our children and grandchildren might sit under them as those farm workers did in generations past.

## Friday — February 3

THIS is the time of year when winter seems to have been around for ever. For some people that feeling reflects times in their lives when any kind of spring seems like a distant impossibility. But the Russians, who surely know a thing or two about winter, have a saying that reminds us that in the darkest days better times are always on their way.

"In the Kingdom of Hope – there is no winter!"

## Saturday — February 4

*CAN it be a new year already?*
*I don't know where the last twelve months went!*
*Most weeks featured something important –*
*A treat or a special event.*
*I spent a long time looking forward –*
*I found myself counting the days*
*To holidays, parties or weddings,*
*The weeks passed me by in a haze.*
*For time, as we know, is so precious –*
*I mustn't waste any amount.*
*I shan't count the days any longer –*
*Instead, I'll make every day count!*

*– Emma Canning.*

## Sunday — February 5

VARIOUS "Rules" on how to live a good life have been handed down to us by pious people from times long gone by. One that caught my eye recently was included in the "Rule of Saint Benedict."

On the subject of how to run a monastery Benedict wrote, "The Abbot should arrange everything so that the strong have something to strive for and the weak should not be disheartened."

Given that each of us will be strong and weak at different times in our lives, that would seem to be advice worth taking out from behind the monastery walls and sharing in our schools, homes and groups of friends.

## Monday — February 6

BEHIND the many roles she played on the silver screen Sophia Loren was also a wife, mother and grandmother. As an Italian, growing up, she liked nothing better than to cook for her family and plenty of kitchen secrets were passed down to her.

But she did make one "secret" public.

"The most indispensable ingredient of all good home cooking," she said, "is love of those you are cooking for."

Whatever it is you do, and whoever it is you do it for, prepare it and serve it up with love.

## Tuesday — February 7

ASKING for help can be difficult and even when we work up the courage we sometimes go all around the houses with our words. As an example, I give you the Lawyer's Prayer. The first part reads:

"We respectively request, and entreat, that due and adequate provisions be made this day and the date hereinafter subscribed, for the organising of such methods and allocations and distributions as may be deemed necessary to properly assure the reception by and for said petitioner of such quantities of baked cereal products as shall, in the judgement of the Provider, constitute a sufficient supply thereof."

It translates as "give us this day our daily bread."

Hopefully, when we receive whatever it is we ask for, we aren't as overly elaborate when it comes to saying, "Thank you!"

## Wednesday — February 8

CAN I just say that you – yes, you – are capable of great things? You might not believe it, but here's what Francis of Assisi said.

"Start by doing what is necessary; then do what is possible, and suddenly you are doing the impossible."

I'm going to start today!

Signs of spring.

## Thursday — February 9

WHAT is your favourite season? I can't decide! Each has its own unique charms. But when the days are short and the weather wet, what is there to recommend winter?

Well, the poet Dame Edith Sitwell had this to say in its defence – "Winter is the time for comfort, for good food and warmth, for the touch of a friendly hand and for a talk beside the fire: it is the time for home."

Everything and everyone has something to recommend it!

## Friday — February 10

HOW would you like to live well? Or perhaps you would like your life to be more concerned with important things like justice and truth? Or maybe a life spent appreciating beauty is more your style.

I'm guessing that the ideal life for most of us would involve a little of all three, which is why the words of the great philosopher Socrates are such good news.

"Living well, and beautifully, and justly," he wrote, "are all one thing."

## Saturday — February 11

NOT much seems to be happening this far after Christmas and New Year. But don't be fooled!

When the days are short it can be easy to settle for a mood as glum as the weather. To counter that I would like to tell you about the Jewish festival of Tu B'Shevat which began last night.

Tu B'Shevat celebrates the New Year of the trees! This is the day the earliest blooming trees in Israel are said to wake from their winter sleep. Tu B'shevat is a reminder that in the dark days when it seems nothing is happening there is usually something wonderful preparing to happen. The preparation can be as much a cause for excitement and celebration as the event itself. Doesn't that thought give the time between the major events in life a little extra charm of their own?

## Sunday — February 12

THE sixth-century monk Dorotheus of Gaza told of a friend who, if he entered a house and found it untidy, would tell himself the owner was obviously too busy with spiritual matters to concern himself with housework. If he entered a house that was spotlessly clean he would tell himself this was a reflection of the owner's soul.

And the people concerned, finding the man thought so well of them, strove to be better; to live up to his image of them.

Might we, by thinking better of people in our lives, do the same?

## Monday — February 13

GEORGE enjoys writing poetry – and he's good at it – but he doubts if it will ever make his name. Why? Because he hates to speak in public. I was able to tell him that Alfred, Lord Tennyson actually resigned from a debating society because he was too nervous to speak in front of an audience.

It's a useful reminder that the "greats" in every field became great by overcoming their difficulties. Now George (who is only ten) is considering the post of future Poet Laureate with renewed interest.

## Tuesday — February 14

*DO you find, as I do, when reading from a book,*
*That there are words that make you stop and take a second look?*
*That lovely word spelled "oily", you can feel it in your mouth;*
*And "zephyr" conjures up those balmy breezes from the south.*
*Then "velvet" – that's another word that I like to repeat,*
*It speaks of warmth in olden days when worn upon the feet.*
*"Sludge" squidges up between your toes when paddling in a river,*
*And "sizzle" smells like sausages, or onions fried with liver!*
*Then "chortle" brings a picture of a baby having fun,*
*And "slither" shows a great, green snake fast-moving in the sun.*
*But of all the words I've come across, the ones that I like best*
*Are "peace" and "love", for these two words mean more than all*
*    the rest.*

– Norah Sinclair.

Perfect presentation.

## Wednesday — February 15

SOME countries are famous for their fertile soil, some have oil or coal in the ground or gold in their hills. A land's natural resources will play a big part in shaping the kind of society that lives on it.

John Muir, a Scotsman who spent his life exploring the American wilderness, wrote, "Storms are never counted among the resources of a country, yet how far they go towards making brave people."

Likewise with the storms we each face from time to time in our lives. We will find ourselves better and stronger for having endured until they passed.

## Thursday — February 16

I ASKED a friend what her hopes and plans for the future were and she replied that her life was so full she just experienced each day as it came. But she planned to do that for all she was worth.

As a fan of planning for the future I was a little taken aback by her response. But the poet Emily Dickinson would surely have agreed with my friend.

She it was who wrote – "To live is so startling it leaves but little room for other occupations."

Perhaps my friend had the right idea – or perhaps there is a middle ground. Might I suggest that we do plan, but that we also plan to be amazed and distracted by life at the same time?

## Friday — February 17

DID you know that in Nepal they have a yearly celebration where they thank dogs for being friends to mankind? The dogs are thanked with garlands of flowers and rewarded with tasty treats.

They are called "man's best friend" after all.

But humanity has always benefited from the company of different animals. Perhaps we can each find a way to thank those pets, and other creatures, who are special to us for all the furry fun they add to our lives.

## Saturday — February 18

TALK of blessings reminded Harry of his dogs. It was a random enough connection, but I have had enough chats with Harry to know the explanation would be forthcoming eventually and it would be a good one.

Harry had discovered a bag of doggy treats in his cupboard. The "use by" wasn't far away so he decided he may as well treat the dogs and use them up.

The retriever, seeing him at the door and hearing the rustling of the packet, came and sat expectantly before him. Harry took a handful of the little treats and threw them over her head on to the patio. The retriever looked up briefly, then, ignoring the treats scattered behind her, focused again on the packet. Another handful was distributed. The retriever looked up and back to the packet. And so on.

"But while she was focused on the packet," Harry explained, "my wee collie was busy eating all the treats behind her! We are constantly being showered by blessings but we sometimes miss them because they don't always arrive in the way we expect them to."

The retriever did, eventually, get some treats. Harry saved her the last handful. She just didn't get as many as the smart little collie, who took his blessings as they arrived – however the one who distributed them chose to send them.

## Sunday — February 19

THE Indian greeting *Namaste* has different levels of meaning, all of which show respect to the person being met. They range from the grand "The divine in me recognises the divine in you" on down to the simple declaration, "Not I, but you."

What would life be like if we all put others before ourselves? Perhaps it might seem like you would always be last in the queue, always be bottom of the pile. But remember, it works both ways. As you put others first, so they also put you first.

Of course, it might make for long delays as we decide who goes through doors first, but I think that might just be a price worth paying!

## Monday — February 20

HAVE you heard of "the greeting of St Francis"? It's said that Francis of Assisi began it and Franciscan monks carried on the tradition. So you might think it would be quite deep and theological. But it's simply this. "Good morning, good people."

Expect the best of the day and the people in it and you will generally not be disappointed.

## Tuesday — February 21

HOW would you like to be a knight or lady of old when the days seemed to be taken up with epic quests and great loves? The modern world doesn't seem to work like that, does it? The daily commute or the school run hardly seems like the exciting journeys of legendary times. There are no dragons to slay or crusades to embark on.

But we can take a tip from the 17th-century monk Brother Lawrence who washed dishes and repaired sandals as offerings of love to God, or the Athenian playwright Euripides who said, "To the generous soul every task is noble."

Now, my noble souls, what shall today's epic quest or act of great love be?

## Wednesday — February 22

TODAY is Scouts' Day, celebrated annually on Robert Baden-Powell's birthday. Lord Baden-Powell set up the Boy Scouts in 1907 and the Girl Guides two years later. Generations of children across the world have grown up in the folds of these organisations, learning skills and principles that have served them well in later life.

A more recent Chief Scout of the Association, the survivalist, adventurer and TV presenter Bear Grylls, was once asked what he thought made the Scout movement so special. He said the principles it espoused reminded him very much of a philosophy his father had passed on to him.

It was simply this – "Follow your dreams and look after your friends."

## Thursday — February 23

**LIKE** dirty car art! The usual is an appeal, apparently from the vehicle to the driver, to "Clean me!"

Now, by gently wiping dirt away, people are creating works of art, stunning landscapes, or dazzling city-scapes, on the sides of vans.

Some of them must take a lot of time and talent, but what I like best about them is the proof, if it was needed, that the human spirit can find, or create, beauty in the most unexpected of places.

And I hold on to that thought – all the way to the car wash!

## Friday — February 24

**HAVE** you ever partaken of an imaginary meal prepared by a child and enjoyed it every bit as much as if it had been cooked by a top chef?

Then you'll know that it isn't the food that makes a meal, it's the enthusiasm with which it is shared and the company that comes with it.

As the old Scots proverb puts it, "Welcome's the best dish in the kitchen." May you enjoy it often. And may you offer it to many.

## Saturday — February 25

*ONE breath of breeze is all it takes*
*To lift your seeds aloft,*
*One breath of breeze on summer days*
*And through the air they waft.*
*One tiny seed is all it takes*
*To drift down straight and true,*
*To find a home – then suddenly*
*Your life's begun anew.*
*Oh, dandelion, some call you "weed"*
*And sigh to see you grow,*
*Yet sad indeed this world would be*
*Without your cheerful glow.*

– Margaret Ingall.

Keeping cosy.

## Sunday — February 26

I ONLY know Antony through social media. He does a fair bit of globe-trotting. Recently he posted that he was in Russia (after being in New Zealand, Australia, Oman, Saudi Arabia and France).

"What on earth are you doing there?" I asked.

"What I do wherever I am," he replied. "Getting to know God better!"

He is a film-maker and his various projects provide the incentive for his travels, but his primary purpose, as he sees it, is always to get to know God better. Nice as it would be to travel for a while, let's not forget that God travels with us wherever we go, even if it's only to the shops. And He's always interested in getting to know us better.

## Monday — February 27

NOT much is known for sure about the life and death of Eckhart von Hochheim, the German monk who lived in the 13th and 14th centuries. But even back in his own lifetime he was known by the respectful title of Meister, or Master.

"Be willing," Meister Eckhart wrote, "to be a beginner every single morning."

The day – each day – will bring its lessons and the way to be master of them is to face them like a beginner – a beginner willing to learn!

## Tuesday — February 28

ANDRÉ GIDE won the Nobel Prize for literature in 1947. Much of his work was autobiographical and dealt with his struggle to find himself in a world that had certain expectations of him.

I wonder if he ever reached any satisfactory conclusion in his search. He may well have. Discussing his work, he said that, "Art is a collaboration between God and the artists, and the less the artist does the better."

Finding yourself has long been a preoccupation of mankind. It might even be the reason we are here. If that's the truth then can I suggest we all collaborate with God, letting Him do what He will with our lives until we find ourselves in the best place possible – in Him.

# March

ON St David's Day, when many will be sporting daffodils, I thought I would share a flower story.

Back in the 1940s a florist ran an ad in "The New York Times". The businessmen who read it couldn't understand it because it was written completely in shorthand, so they asked their secretaries to translate. The cheeky ad was actually addressed to those secretaries, asking them to remember Max Schling's florist shop when their boss's wife's birthday came around.

He spoke to them in a language they would understand. And Schling also understood flowers.

"The love of flowers," he once said, "is really the best teacher of how to grow and understand them."

Love of any subject, topic or person is surely the best way to help them grow and to help us understand. It's a simple and obvious truth. But sometimes these truths are so obvious we need to be reminded of them.

If only I could have written it in shorthand!

AFTER a hard day many of us fall into bed with a sigh of relief, but how many of us think to count beds among our blessings? The great diarist Samuel Pepys certainly did!

"And mighty proud I am," he wrote, "and ought to be thankful to God Almighty, that I am able to have a spare bed for my friends."

Easily pleased? But a bed where one might sleep safely and comfortably is a wonderful thing, especially in a time when many slept on straw-filled mattresses on the floor. To have two – and friends willing to sleep on the other one – is a blessing indeed.

A spare bed – friends – what other normally overlooked blessings could we add to the list? I'm going to sleep on it!

## Friday — March 3

W E'VE had a flash of sunlight – a crisp, cold frosty day,
A lovely, sparkling diamond nestling in dark clouds of grey,
A welcome intermission during days of wintry showers
When you hardly dare to blink in case you miss the daylight hours.
We've had a day of sunshine, oh, the joy of sun again,
It lifts the weary spirit so beleaguered by the rain
And serves as a reminder that spring's coming by and by . . .
Yes, how it cheers the heart to see a beautiful blue sky!
We've had a flash of sunlight – and now the day is done,
The evening sky is set on fire by a huge red glowing sun,
Nature's parting gift to us so that our eyes might see
The richness of God's heaven, waiting there for you and me!

– Marian Cleworth

## Saturday — March 4

T HE ability to count is such an important attribute in life that
we teach it to toddlers in nursery rhymes. There will be sound
benefits that come from being able to count, but perhaps we could
multiply those benefits if we thought more carefully about what we
counted.

Which is why I wanted to share this poem by our old friend
A. Nonymous –

Count your blessings instead of your crosses;

Count your gains instead of your losses.

Count your joys instead of your woes;

Count your friends instead of your foes.

Count your smiles instead of your tears;

Count your courage instead of your fears.

Count your full years instead of your lean;

Count your kind deeds instead of your mean.

Count your health instead of your wealth;

Count on God instead of yourself.

## Sunday — March 5

**DO** like it when a hymn seems to speak to me. But one wag suggested there was a hymn for everyone. Such as –

- Crown Him With Many Crowns for dentists
- Open My Eyes That I Might See for opticians
- There Is A Green Hill Far Away for golfers

And the hymn for those folk filling in their tax returns – I Surrender All.

It's frivolous, of course, but it reminds me that very few hymns were written by professional songwriters. Some were written by ministers but many were written by ordinary people, trying to express an extraordinary relationship.

By all means sing your own song to God. But if you can't come up with your own then there will undoubtedly be one out there somewhere that seems like it was written especially for you.

## Monday — March 6

**THE** Danish pianist Victor Borge, who was regularly distracted from the next classical piece he wanted to play by the urgent need to tell his audience a funny story – all as part of the act, of course – once said, "Laughter is the shortest distance between two people."

When people laugh together the things that separate them, like race, creed and status, disappear. They have found a common ground, found that it is good, and they are instantly closer together.

## Tuesday — March 7

**IF** you took all the supposed words of wisdom that begin with the words, "There are two kinds of people . . ." you would be forgiven for thinking there must be endless numbers of different kinds of people in the world.

I prefer the novelist Harper Lee's take on the subject.

"I think there's just one kind of folks," she wrote. "Folks."

## Wednesday — March 8

ACCORDING to an old Arabian proverb, "A fig tree looking upon another fig tree becomes fruitful."

We could look at those words prosaically, saying, well, apple trees need other apple trees to help them pollinate. But I think it's all about the power of a good example. In other words, the one tree sees another tree growing a fine crop of fruit and follows suit.

Of course, trees don't think that way. But proverbs aren't meant for trees.

Live your life in such a way that others seeing you will aspire to your example. Bear good fruit through your everyday behaviour and others, seeing that, will want to do the same.

## Thursday — March 9

THERE'S an old saying that the smile you send out into the world will return to you. It's easily said, but how easy is it to do in real life? Some people in some circumstances might seem undeserving of our smiles.

And there's the challenge! Because if you can find it in yourself to offer them a smile, the effect it has might surprise you. If nothing else you will have made yourself a better person. And the smile you get back (if you do get one back), coming from such an unexpected source, might warm your heart for a week!

## Friday — March 10

A GOOD laugh is great – but how seriously should we take it? Author Garrison Keillor thinks it keeps some pretty exalted company.

"Humour is a presence in the world," he said. "Like grace. And shines on everybody."

He was not talking about jokes, tricks or laughing at people. Just plain old good humour. When we share it with someone, he seemed to think – and I agree – we are sharing more than just a laugh.

IN days long gone by, a woman was expected to be proficient in several domestic skills to prove her worthiness as a wife. Needlework was one of the most important skills – and certainly one of the ones most likely to be used.

Apparently, it was a tradition in some places for the bride-to-be to stitch twelve quilts in the year before her wedding, with the last one being for the marital bed.

And the other eleven? They were usually given away to the families of the women who helped her with the task, perhaps by providing materials. Which probably meant that a lot of children slept cosier because of the tradition.

Times have certainly changed since then and a whole different set of skills are needed these days. But it's still a sign of a good marriage that it blesses and "warms" more than just the happy couple.

## Sunday — March 12

*SHOULD today be the tomorrow*
*That concerned you yesterday,*
*Of all the days that really count,*
*That one should be today.*
*So think not on the morrow,*
*For it has yet to come,*
*And that imposter, yesterday,*
*Is over and is done.*

*So if the present troubles you*
*And you have lost the way,*
*Entrust it to the will of God,*
*And simply kneel and pray.*
*For one thing that is certain,*
*No matter time nor tide,*
*There are no circumstances*
*He will ever leave your side.*

– Brian H. Gent.

## Monday — March 13

IN 1766 Captain Samuel Wallace circumnavigated the globe at the helm of *HMS Dolphin*. Two years later Captain Cook performed the same feat on board the *HMS Endeavour*. John Gore was Master's Mate on the first voyage and Third Lieutenant on the second.

But another "sailor" made both journeys to much less acclaim.

A goat, known simply as the Goat, provided the officers with fresh milk on both voyages. So much was her contribution appreciated that Captain Cook had a silver collar made for her and retired her to the grounds of his home.

This is a useful reminder that great ventures often depend as much on the contributions of the humblest servants as they do on the efforts of their glorious leaders.

## Tuesday — March 14

BE somebody! Surprisingly enough, I'm not encouraging you to become famous or influential. I just don't want you to be nobody.

Samuel Smiles, the 19th-century moralist, wrote, "That terrible Nobody! How much has he to answer for? More mischief is done by Nobody than by all the world besides!"

Be famous, if you like. Be influential. But be the person who takes responsibility for their actions and make as many of those as possible good ones. Be somebody. Don't be Nobody!

## Wednesday — March 15

PUBLISHED in 1653, Izaak Walton's book was called "The Compleat Angler". So why did Mr Walton rate the lifestyle of the angler so highly? Because while others were occupied by "important" matters, the angler gets to "sit on cowslip-banks, hear the birds sing, and possess ourselves in as much quietness as the silver streams, which we now see glide so quietly by us."

Sounds like a lifestyle worth seeking out and one I am sure anglers still enjoy today when they can. As for the rest of us, well, I am sure we can find some excuse to sit on a cowslip-bank for a while.

Kidding around!

## Thursday — March 16

I N the 1954 film version of J.B. Priestley's "An Inspector Calls", Eric, the son of a wealthy businessman, finds himself unexpectedly on a tram. Discovering that he doesn't have tuppence for his fare, he is temporarily at a loss.

When the young woman sitting next to him buys his ticket he tries to find a way to repay her, but she insists it doesn't matter.

"Well, of course it matters," he replies. "It's just these little things that do matter."

He doesn't always acquit himself so wisely in life or in the rest of the film, but at that moment Eric gets it just right.

The journey through life, be it by tram or any other means, is turned from something mundane into something altogether more wonderful, not by great acts, but by one tuppenny ticket, or little act of kindness, after another.

Those are what really matter.

## Friday — March 17

I T'S years, I know – so long ago –
  Yet I'd never forget: I knew you'd be
The one for me the moment that we met.

Trustworthy, kind – a joy to find –
You brought a wealth of pleasure;
And fondness grew swiftly into a love to hold and treasure.

When you and I were challenged by
Storms that seemed hard to weather,
Secure we stayed, staunch; unafraid; we faced those storms
    together.

And now, steadfast, though years have passed,
We live so happily. And still it's true
That next to you is where I love to be.

– Emma Canning

## Saturday — March 18

HOME is a difficult thing to define and this little story doesn't help much with that – but it is charming!

A friend's grandparents made the trek across Europe to freedom during World War II. They took only what they could carry, so the cases were packed with essentials and the cloth from the table at home where the family ate dinner. Wherever they stopped, be it a riverbank, a barn or under a bridge, Mother would unpack the tablecloth and spread it out over her suitcase. That makeshift dinner table became home to the children gathered around it.

What one item would speak of home for you, wherever you were?

## Sunday — March 19

HARRY had a fabulous holiday in Brazil. Of course, he had to take the cable car up Sugarloaf Mountain and photograph the massive, and very impressive, statue of Christ the Redeemer.

It was only when he looked at it later that he realised there were other tourists included in the photo. They had Jesus behind them while photographing the spectacular view of Rio de Janeiro.

"I'm sure they photographed the statue as well," Harry told me. "But the image was a powerful reminder of how we let the world distract us from what really matters."

## Monday — March 20

AS spring officially begins (no matter what the weather may be like outside) I'd like to share some thoughts about the season.

Alfred, Lord Tennyson, famously wrote, "In the spring a young man's fancy lightly turns to thoughts of love." American writer Hamilton Wright Mabie said, "Blessed is the season which engages the whole world in a conspiracy of love."

And what do I have to offer? Only this! That spring may be holding its end up, but if summer, autumn and winter aren't also seasons of love then they're just not trying hard enough.

Let's see what we can do about that, shall we?

## Tuesday — March 21

THE Vigil of Venus is a poem in praise of the goddess of Love and sees her influence in the arrival of spring, and there is at least one line in it that is just as applicable today as it was then. In preparation for the coming season, it encourages its listeners, "Now learn ye to love who loved never – now ye who have loved, love anew."

Spring is unquestionably a time of rebirth. What better time, whatever your past experience, to begin again? And what better way to begin again than in love? And the same holds true for every day of the year.

Love, of course, has one advantage over spring. It doesn't have to die to be reborn. A look or a smile can take care of that!

## Wednesday — March 22

LEGEND has it that King Cyrus of Persia tamed a mighty river by damming and diverting so much that it almost disappeared. The once-mighty torrent no longer powered its way directly to the sea, but provided drinking water and sanitation and irrigated the endless acres of crops needed to feed the Persian people.

The river's identity almost ceased to exist but the good it did was multiplied beyond measure.

So it goes with people also. When we worry less about what we might be for our own sakes and think more about what we might be for the sake of others, we might diminish our fame (in the conventional sense) but we will get so much more good stuff done.

## Thursday — March 23

IDEALLY, our family will be the one we were born into. But it might be a group of friends, people who have been through the same experiences as you, or people brought together by love.

The author Jane Howard wrote, "Call it a clan, call it a tribe, call it a family. Whatever you call it, whoever you are, you need one."

As the actor Michael J. Fox pointed out, "Family is not an important thing. It is everything!"

Glorious sunset.

## Friday — March 24

IN these days of instant communications it can be easy to get into arguments. John Newton, who wrote "Amazing Grace", lived when communications were slower and had advice on the matter that might still be usefully applied.

"You will be met with three types of response," he wrote. "Those who disagree on principle; those who will readily approve of what you say; and a third who will be influenced by the writer's spirit."

In other words, the only thing that will make a difference is our attitude. Whether it's by letter, online or face to face, we should remember to take the right spirit with us in all our interactions.

And, if we can, make it the spirit of love.

## Saturday — March 25

MOST of us will have feelings of inadequacy from time to time. In response to a poem her husband wrote in praise of her, Willa Muir said, "I am only a botched version of what I was meant to be."

But to her husband, Edwin Muir, Willa was as a place of rest to a lost traveller, and the wonderful lens through which he saw Creation.

We can be our own worst critics, but just as Willa was perfect for Edwin so you and I, while not perfect in our own eyes, will be as God made us. Perfect in His eyes, and worthy of a rhyming couplet or two!

## Sunday — March 26

IN the first verse of the old Scottish nursery rhyme, Wee Willie Winkie isn't a mischevious child as is commonly thought, he is the personification of sleep. The rest of the rhyme consists of a tired mother pleading for him to visit. You see, her baby prefers to tease the cat, rattle the pots, cry loud enough to wake the neighbours!

But, exhausted as she is, "ae kiss frae aff his rosy lips gi'es strength anew to me." It seems love is the energy that keeps a mother going, so if you get the chance this Mothering Sunday, why not recharge your mother's batteries with a kiss – without all the preceding nonsense, of course!

## Monday — March 27

THE picture is supposed to show isolation and separation, but my ten-year-old great-nephew had a different take on it.

Two men stand on opposite sides of a chasm. Previously, the only way across the chasm had been a single rope to which I imagine brave souls must have clung very tightly. But at some point (and hopefully with no-one on it at the time) it had snapped. Each man now only had half the rope and no way to get across, hence the isolation and separation.

The young Adam said, "One man unties his rope and throws it to the other. That man ties both ropes together and throws one end back. Both end up sharing a whole rope – but someone has to give his away first."

If each kept what they had then neither of them got anywhere. But if someone gives all he has – in trust – then everyone benefits. Now, how many ways can we apply that theory to life and the world in general?

## Tuesday — March 28

I AM never surprised when our dear friend Mary gives a less than standard answer to a standard question. But when I asked how she was some time back and she replied, "Oh, just daisying on," I did have to enquire further.

"It was a rose bush I was looking at, Francis," she explained. "The roses were lovely, but from the middle of the bush and standing a few inches clear of the blooms sprouted a daisy! It had obviously started to grow in the shade underneath the rose bush. Not the most hospitable environment. Its slender stalk kept growing, undaunted by the thorns, undeterred by the branches, and caring not a whit for the more conventionally famous flowers. It just grew through and past all of that towards the sunshine, being the best daisy it could be. Just . . . daisying on!"

She's more of a rare bloom than a common garden flower, is our Mary. But now, whenever I hear of someone beating the odds by ignoring them and simply doing their best regardless, I can't help but say softly, "Daisy on, my friend. Daisy on."

Joy of spring.

## Wednesday — March 29

KONSTANTIN was on his way to propose to Kitty in Tolstoy's novel, "Anna Karenina". Walking through the waking city, he was entranced by ordinary things.

"Those loaves," he said to himself, "the pigeons, the two little boys, seemed not of this earth." Love can do that for you!

The question we need to ask is whether love changes those ordinary things, or whether it helps us see them as they really are. And if it is the latter, the next challenge is to see the ordinary as wonderful not just when we are in love but every day of our lives.

Because if the world really is like that – and I believe it is – it would be a shame to miss even one day of it.

## Thursday — March 30

YOU wouldn't expect me to encourage you to talk about people behind their backs. Most of the people who do it have nothing nice to say.

There is an old proverb that says, "They are good friends that speak well of us behind our backs."

By all means, talk about people when they aren't there – and use it as another opportunity to build them up. You don't have to worry about them hearing what you said. In fact, you can be sure that if they do hear what you said about them they will be delighted!

## Friday — March 31

IN his 17th-century publication "Jacula Prudentium", the poet and priest George Herbert gives us a list of wise sayings and private thoughts. One I particularly liked was this. "He quits his place well," Herbert wrote, "who leaves a friend behind."

By "quitting his place" Herbert may have meant leaving this life or, perhaps, leaving a place of employment. But might we make our place wherever we happen to be? Then we could quit that place well, assured that if ever we returned there would be someone there who would be glad to welcome us back.

# April

## Saturday — April 1

CAROLANNE is part of a community choir. They visit care homes, support good causes, and sing for the love of it. The choir was performing in a hall in her home town and all the family turned out, including her three-year-old granddaughter, Evie.

When the choir had reached a particularly resounding crescendo and lapsed into a momentary silence, Evie jumped up on her chair and shouted, "Well done, Grandma!"

As far as little Evie was concerned her grandma was making the beautiful music all by herself, and she was doing a good job!

It's all too easy in this busy, noisy world to imagine you are lost in the crowd, that no-one notices what you do. But it isn't true. Someone is watching you like Evie watched her grandma. He will see you in any crowd and He wants to tell you, "Well done!"

So sing a little louder, live a little brighter. To that someone you are the star of the show.

## Sunday — April 2

WRITING about education, the poet John Milton declared it should have two purposes: to enable people to perform their duties "justly, skilfully, and magnanimously" and to enable them to "know God aright and out of that knowledge to love Him and be as like Him as we may."

He also believed there was much to be learned in the natural world – especially at this time of year.

"In those vernal seasons of the year," he wrote, "when the air is calm and pleasant, it were an injury and sullenness against nature not to go out and see her riches and partake in her rejoicing."

Of course, Milton had a point. When spring has gone to so much effort to bring beauty back into God's world, it would be rude not to appreciate it.

## Monday — April 3

POLLY is just back from a week in Prague and couldn't wait to tell me about the National Netherlands building, home to a major insurance company. She told me it was also known as the Dancing House and sometimes referred to as the Fred and Ginger Building.

You see, the building is in two parts; one is tall and straight, while the other seems to sway and lean in on its partner for support. Standing out as they do from all the other buildings, the twin parts of this one actually seem to be dancing.

"It was like one of your philosophies for life," she told me. "Be strong and upright when you need to be, but always be prepared to sway when the opportunity presents itself."

Or, as Fred sang to Ginger, when life is troublesome, "Let's face the music and dance."

## Tuesday — April 4

WHAT is the best thing a friend can do for you in difficult times? Get involved? Perhaps. But sometimes simply the knowledge that you have a friend who will happily come to your aid is enough to give you the strength to carry on.

As the Greek philosopher Epicurus wrote, "It is not so much our friends' help that helps us, as the confidence of their help."

## Wednesday — April 5

*IF we are afraid of what the future has in store,*
*It helps to focus on today. One thing we know for sure:*
*A day that's lost in brooding, fearful of a future sorrow*
*Will not ease any plight or pain that may arrive tomorrow.*
*And when it seems that every anxious moment lasts for ever*
*And conquering each task is such a difficult endeavour,*
*Remember, the view from the top is always worth the climb,*
*And that the future comes to us just one day at a time.*

– Emma Canning.

## Thursday — April 6

THE term "April showers" didn't come into being for no reason. April is usually a well-watered month, but the lush growth that follows is worth getting wet for occasionally.

The 1864 Book Of Days had this to say – "April is beautiful to look upon; and if she hides her sweet face for a few hours behind the rainclouds it is only so that she might appear again peeping out through the next burst of sunshine in a veil of fresher green."

This green and pleasant land does need rain to keep it that way. So, let's not grudge April her showers. And if we find cloudy times in our lives let us do what she does – retire for a while only to reappear, refreshed, with the next burst of sunshine.

## Friday — April 7

THE Earl of Winchilsea once offended the Duke of Wellington. The Iron Duke demanded satisfaction, which meant a duel. Taking pity on his opponent, the duke shot first and deliberately shot wide.

The earl discharged his pistol into the sky and later wrote a public apology for the initial offence.

Sometimes when you are entitled to retribution it is a braver action not to claim it. The example of a higher way might just turn the enemy you could have beaten into a friend who would stand by you.

## Saturday — April 8

VISITORS to the Tower of London might stop in Sir Walter Raleigh's cell, where the main feature is a beautifully carved writing desk.

Imprisoned there for 14 years on a charge of treason, Raleigh passed his time writing beautiful poetry and compiling a history of the world.

Many of us will find ourselves in situations we would rather not be in from time to time. Do we stare at the walls or do we look beyond and put our unexpected situation to some wonderful use?

## Sunday — April 9

THE Church of Saint Michael and All Angels in East Sussex is a beautiful building. But the windows to the north and the south of the church were blown in during the bombing of World War II and replaced by plain glass.

The official reasons given for this are that new stained glass would have cost too much and they weren't sure there wouldn't be more bombing. But maybe someone looked out through those windows at the beautiful South Downs and understood that all man's artistry couldn't begin to compare with God's handiwork.

## Monday — April 10

JOHN of the Cross was a reforming Carmelite monk in 16th-century Spain. You might think he would have nothing in common with the thousands who travel to his homeland every year in modern times to let their hair down and have a wild time.

But John knew about having a good time. His way was perhaps the more meaningful one, involving no hangover, and you didn't have to go back to work afterwards.

"The soul of the person who loves God," he wrote, "is always swimming in joy, always on holiday, and always in the mood for singing!"

## Tuesday — April 11

THEY say you can have too much of a good thing.

In the Bible, when the Israelites complained of eating manna every day, God sent them quail, a luxury food, until they were sick of it. In 1888 a Mrs Titus bet Mr Titus she could eat one broiled quail every day for thirty days. The bet was for a large sum of cash and a diamond ring. She won – but apparently she never claimed her prize. Perhaps she had had enough of the rich life.

A life of only the exotic, the delicious, the expensive, without the humble things: nice for a while, to be sure, but for always? Why, I quail at the very thought!

## Wednesday — April 12

WE probably all know what Neil Armstrong said when he landed on the moon. "One small step for man . . ." and all that. But how many remember what Yuri Gagarin, the first man to go into space, said when he looked out of his space craft?

"I see Earth," he gasped on this day in 1961. "It is so beautiful!"

And it still is. Those of us who aren't cosmonauts or astronauts won't have the advantage of Gagarin's spectacular viewpoint, but at least we get to see it close up!

So, let's take the time to appreciate it anew.

## Thursday — April 13

MAUNDY Thursday has become known to many as the day the monarch of the realm distributes alms, or Maundy money.

But what does the word Maundy actually mean?

Well, it is a shortened version of the Latin phrase *mandatum novum do vobis*, which translates as, "A new commandment I give unto you."

And that commandment was to love one another as God loves us!

It's an idea worth remembering and putting into practice, on Maundy Thursday and every other day of the year.

## Friday — April 14

DID you ever play with a kaleidoscope?

The early ones used tiny polished stones and broken pieces of coloured glass. But the careful positioning of the mirrors made them into wonderful patterns.

Broken objects and things worn smooth by abrasion – seen as beautiful because the viewer looked at them in a particular way. But, really, wasn't the beauty always there?

Now, if only we can learn to look at worn and broken people the same way. Through the kaleidoscope of love, perhaps?

## Saturday — April 15

JUST as the world seems to be blossoming again, a late frost can often appear. That's the wonder of the British weather. Anything can happen at any time!

Then the early blossoms can find themselves frost-nipped before they have properly opened. Plants that are "nipped in the bud" rarely come to anything. So much so that the term has come into the language as signifying something that gets stopped before it gets properly started.

The weather – especially in April – might be unpredictable, but you and I can be counted on for more stability and civility.

If we see someone trying to do better or attempting to improve something, let's not bring it to a halt with a frosty look or word. Let's add our own personal sunshine and watch it grow.

## Sunday — April 16

THINK of an Easter earthquake and some might recall the Gospel account of the earth shaking when Jesus died. All nature is supposed to have grieved, dead prophets came back to life and the Temple veil was ripped asunder. Of course the end result, three days later, was new life!

Julie, who works in a hospital, said she heard what sounded like an earthquake as she began her shift, so she looked outside.

It wasn't an earthquake. It was the annual visit of a group of local bikers as they came to deliver hundreds of Easter eggs to the children's wards.

And how did the tradition begin, I asked. Did one of them have a child in hospital and was inspired to help other children?

"I don't think so," she said. "I think it's just because they're a really nice bunch of guys."

Bless their hearts. Such kindness, from what some might regard as an unlikely source, is surely enough to bring new life to even the most jaded of hearts.

Thunder like that I could do with hearing more often!

Spring idyll.

## Monday — April 17

AS the author of several books (which provided the basis for the "Little House On The Prairie" TV series) Laura Ingalls Wilder was obviously good with words. She even had an opinion on which one was the nicest. According to her, "Home is the nicest word there is."

We can take her word for it. As well as the little house on the prairie, she had about fifteen of them in her life, many of them hard-won and all of them looked back on with affection, so she certainly knew what she was talking about.

Home! It may be a stately mansion, a draughty, cold shack; it may not be all it should be, or it may be more . . . but which of us can say the word without that ever so slight warming of the heart?

## Tuesday — April 18

THE great actor Sir Ralph Richardson was almost as famous for his wit as he was for his acting ability. He once described his work on the stage as "the art of keeping people from coughing."

But he also gave some serious acting advice which those of us who don't tread the boards might take into our everyday life.

"The most precious things in speech," he said, "are pauses."

For actors those pauses help build dramatic effect. For you and me they provide a chance to listen; a moment to allow someone else to be centre stage.

## Wednesday — April 19

BETWEEN three and five hundred years before Christ, the city-state of Athens was a major supporter and provider of the arts and philosophy as well as the dominant military power in the area. These days that city is referred to as the cradle of western civilisation.

The philosopher Plato said, "This city is what it is because its citizens are what they are."

What applied to the city-state also applies to the state, and the city, and the town, the village, the home, and the family. If we would change society we must begin with us.

## Thursday — April 20

*THERE'S surely no more lazy sound*
*than busy, buzzing bees,*
*All heads down in the lavender*
*That perfumes every breeze.*
*It's odd to think that boffins rule*
*That bees just shouldn't fly,*
*That bumblebees' wings are too short*
*To lift them to the sky.*
*But Mother Nature, old and wise,*
*Who made both whales and fleas,*
*Decided, in her clever way,*
*She wouldn't tell the bees!*

– Eileen Hay.

## Friday — April 21

MY new neighbours were difficult to love," Harry admitted. "So I took C.S. Lewis's advice."

The author of the Narnia books once said, "Don't waste time wondering if you love your neighbour: act as if you do."

Harry said it wasn't easy at first.

"But," he said, "the more I put that advice into action, the more they seemed to like me. And the more difficult I found it not to love people with such good taste in neighbours!"

Harry's obvious happiness reminded me of another old saying: "Where there is no love, put love – and there you will find love!"

## Saturday — April 22

HELEN GURLEY BROWN was the international editor of "Cosmopolitan" magazine. She rose as far as it was possible in her chosen profession and her advice to others seeking to do the same was, "Work with the raw materials you have – namely you!"

It might not seem like much but none of the truly great names in history ever had any more.

## Sunday — April 23

THE classic legend has St George as a knight in armour, saving a beautiful, innocent young maiden from a marauding dragon.

It's a noble and stirring image, but knights in armour are history while dragons are, happily, mythological creatures.

Another version of the story, perhaps more grounded in reality, has George being a Roman soldier at a time before Christianity was adopted by the empire. Seen as a traitor for refusing to acknowledge the Emperor as God, he was imprisoned and tortured for his Christianity. The beautiful and innocent thing he "saved" was his faith which he refused to deny and eventually died for.

Not much more is known about him but his sacrifice was enough to inspire England, Georgia, Malta and Gozo to adopt him as their patron saint.

If you would honour St George today, on his national holiday, then don't go looking for dragons to fight. Instead, choose to stand for something worthwhile and defend it steadfastly.

## Monday — April 24

I DO like it when we can take inspiration from God's creation but I was confused when Bill suggested that waterfalls might be role models.

"Think about it," Bill said, determined to educate me. "The river rolls along, gently for the most part. Sure, there are a few rocks, a few bumps and boulders like most of us experience in our lives. Then the ground seems to be whipped away from underneath it!

"It falls suddenly, hitting the bottom in a white foam of confusion. What does it do next? Does it waste time complaining about what happened? Does it get frustrated because it can't get back up that hill to where it was before? No. The river gathers itself together and flows on, smoothly and serenely, doing what it did before, only in a new place. As if the fall never happened."

Tumbling over waterfalls also aerates rivers, making them healthier places to live in. Bill's words of wisdom often do the same to my brain!

## Tuesday — April 25

THE great composer Ludwig van Beethoven enjoyed success in his lifetime but his personal life was far from happy. His mother died young and his father descended into drink. His hearing started to fail while still in his twenties and he was often ill for extended periods.

But to compose such beautiful music, of a kind that has inspired and comforted many generations and will doubtless continue to do so, he must have been in touch with some greater truth; he must have known happiness at an essential level.

So we should take his advice when he said, "Love, and love alone, is capable of giving thee a happier life."

Love, after all, is a melody any of us can compose and a tune we all can play.

## Wednesday — April 26

A PHILOSOPHY for life would surely be a good thing. But Eleanor Roosevelt didn't necessarily agree.

"I have never given very deep thought to a philosophy of life," she said, "though I do have a few ideas that I think are useful to me. One is that you do whatever comes your way as well as you can, and another is that you think as little as possible of yourself and as much as possible about other people. The third is that you get more joy out of giving joy to others and should put a good deal of thought into the happiness that you are able to give."

Isn't it funny how a few ideas in lieu of a philosophy can end up being so wonderfully philosophical?

## Thursday — April 27

JEAN-BAPTISTE ALPHONSE KARR was a journalist who said every man had three characters – "That which he exhibits, that which he has, and that which he thinks he has."

It's worth considering, because happiness surely lies in having the one character: the one we wanted, the one we achieved, and the one we are happy to share with the world.

## Friday — April 28

THE very talented actress Meryl Streep was once told she was too ugly for a film role. She told the director that his was just one opinion in a sea of opinions and she was "off to find a kinder tide."

Some tides in the oceans will beat you down while others will soothe your soul. People are like that, too. Meryl Streep refused to stay where she would be beaten down, and she went on to win three Academy Awards.

Stay away from the "rip-currents" of life and find a tide that will raise you up to all that you can be.

## Saturday — April 29

LIFE is mostly froth and bubble. Two things stand like stone. Kindness in another's trouble. Courage in your own."

These are the more famous lines from "Ye Wearie Wayfarer" by the 19th-century Australian poet Adam Lindsay Gordon. But I would like to bring to greater notice, if I might, the lines that precede them.

The "wearie" traveller wonders if his goal is near but, "In my ear the wind that whispers, Seems to make reply, 'Question not, but live and labour 'til yon goal be won. Helping every feeble neighbour, seeking help from none'."

Wonderful sentiments, and I would only take issue with one item. Let us not be afraid or ashamed to accept help. After all, others will want to be good neighbours, too!

## Sunday — April 30

I'M always quietly pleased to see prayer rooms in places like busy airports. But they remind me of the time a TV producer set aside a private room for Billy Graham to pray in before an interview. An aide told him it wouldn't be needed because, "Mr Graham started praying when he got up this morning, he prayed on the way over in the car, and he'll probably be praying all the way through the interview."

A life of constant prayer needn't look any different from any other. It just needs to be spent in God's company. We are never anywhere else. We just need to remember it.

# May

*I LOVE to walk along the beach*
*Beside the crashing waves.*
*Above me seagulls soar to reach*
*Their homes in distant caves.*
*Rolling tides remove all trace*
*Of children's games from view.*
*And in my mind I'm like the sand,*
*Washed clean and good as new.*

– Flo Jones.

HARRY tells me he likes to listen to music as he showers. He has an old waterproof radio in the shape of a frog that sits on a shelf in the bathroom. (Are you blushing yet, Harry?)

But Froggy is getting old and the radio reception in that part of the house has never been great. Harry was singing along to a favourite tune as he got dried recently. Donning his dressing-gown, he walked into his bedroom – and the music cut out. He returned to the bathroom and it came back on again.

"It was like I had to be there for the signal to get through," he told me, shaking his head in wonder.

I thought about it for a moment.

"I've always said that we never really know the good we are doing simply by being where we are, but I wasn't thinking about radio reception."

"I suppose," Harry said, "if I am going to be an aerial then I ought to make sure I only receive the best signals."

We both wondered what kind of signals we might pick up and pass on, and what good we might do wherever we are just by being there – then I suggested he might get Froggy some new batteries as well.

## Wednesday — May 3

A SECRET garden is a beautiful idea. Which of us hasn't, at one time or another, longed to find such a place; a haven of peace, cared for by a loving gardener who is nowhere to be seen and who doesn't mind us relaxing as we enjoy the results of his hard work?

Frances Hodgson Burnett, who wrote the classic children's story, "The Secret Garden", had a beautiful walled garden of her own where she used to write when she wasn't weeding and pruning. But she understood how each of us might find such a place regardless of our circumstances.

"If you look the right way," she wrote, "you can see that the whole world is a garden."

## Thursday — May 4

I SAW a woman sweeping glass from an all-weather pitch. Some teenagers, who had perhaps contributed to the mess, were standing nearby.

"Why are you cleaning this for them to use when they are laughing at you?" I asked.

"They aren't all laughing," she told me. "Some are watching."

I looked again and it was true. Perhaps we can't reach the scoffers, but the quiet watchers are always there. Set your example for those who will see it.

## Friday — May 5

OF course, there are good words beginning with "un". Unbroken, for instance. Or unfailing. But, in general, the "un" words tend to be unfortunate, unlovely ones, always busy not being something.

When the poet E.E. Cummings wrote to a friend on the occasion of the friend's wedding, he said, "Joy is by far the rarest thing in or out of any world. Joy isn't un-anything. Joy IS."

My advice for this fine day? Don't be "un". Find your joy, and get busy being!

Time for a break . . .

## Saturday — May 6

JOSEPH CAMPBELL spent most of his life studying what different cultures believed: their religions, their myths, legends and heroes. These, he was sure, played a big part in how successful or otherwise that culture was.

His scholarly work was detailed and his conclusions many and complex, but one little nugget of wisdom from all of that did particularly appeal to me.

"We cannot cure the world of its sorrows," he wrote, "but we can choose to live in joy."

Given that joy tends to make more joy, if we kept making that decision we might eventually find that most of those sorrows seemed to happen "a long time ago in a galaxy far away".

## Sunday — May 7

THOSE who travel by ship can easily find themselves blown off course. They look for some beacon or high peak that is easy to identify. Once they have found it they can set a new course to the harbour they seek."

Gregory of Nyssa had Scripture in mind for his beacon or high peak guiding the travellers to the harbour of heaven. But until then, those of us who have travelled the metaphorical seas of life and found our own harbour might still shine the light of experience, letting those who are still buffeted by turbulent waters know there is a happy and contented landfall that's worth turning their sails towards.

## Monday — May 8

CURIOSITY took the poet John Keats to Scotland in the early 19th century. But when he got there he found –

"That the ground was as hard, that a yard was as long
That a song was as merry, that a cherry was as red . . .
So, he stood in his shoes and he wondered."

Might it be that in the whole world over, there are more things that unite us than separate us?

HOW would you like to be an artist?

Well, assuming you aren't one already, the first step would be to find someone to teach you how it's done. We would all like to have the very best, the expert in the field, as a tutor but they aren't often available.

Sometimes, however, we can learn from their advice. Which is why I wanted to share with you some words Vincent van Gogh wrote to his brother, Theo, about art.

These days a van Gogh painting is likely to be amongst the most expensive in the world. Back then only Theo was buying them.

"I tell you," he wrote, "the more I think about it the more I feel that there is nothing more truly artistic than to love people." As his brother's sole supporter I am sure Theo understood that, even if he couldn't put it into words.

Want to be a great artist? Love people!

## Wednesday — May 10

FROM far-flung lands you came here
In days now long gone past,
You stayed, and now you give us
Your splendour unsurpassed.
Magnolia pure and perfect,
Your annual show's sublime,
Though each year newly minted,
Your roots stretch back through time,
Your history is ancient,
Both ice and flood you've known,
As continents divided
You've still survived and grown.
May long you stay tenacious,
May long you ever thrive!
And may, when'er we see you,
Feel glad to be alive.

– Margaret Ingall.

## Thursday — May 11

JAMES THOMSON was a Scottish poet and musician who lived in the 18th century. A poem of his declares that, "Among the changing months, May stands confest the sweetest, and in fairest colours dressed."

He also wrote, "But who can paint like Nature? Can imagination boast, Amid its gay creation, hues like hers?"

The British weather isn't the most predictable but I could wish that this May lives up to that beautiful description. Human nature isn't the most predictable, either, but we could do a lot worse than to aspire to follow the example of James Thomson's appreciation.

## Friday — May 12

FRIENDSHIP? Or falling in love? Which is best? Well, I wouldn't dare venture an opinion!

The author of "Wuthering Heights", Emily Brontë, turned to the natural world for this charming comparison – "Love is like the wild rose-briar, friendship like the holly-tree. The holly is dark when the rose-briar blooms, But which will bloom most constantly?"

To which I would only add that holly and briar-roses each bring something unique to the natural world and it would be poorer without either one of them. Likewise with friendship and love.

## Saturday — May 13

KARLE (also known as Charlotte) Wilson Baker wrote, among many beautiful poems, one called "Good Company". It includes the line, "Today I have grown taller from walking with the trees."

There truly is nothing like a walk in the woods to reconnect with yourself. Those trees, it seemed to Karle, were firmly rooted in this world but always reaching for the world above.

For those of us who don't have easy access to woodland walks, the same effect can come from spending time with people we admire. Spend enough time in their company and you might notice another "woodland walker" wanting to spend time with you.

A walk in the wood.

## Sunday — May 14

**B**ISHOP BERNARD OF CLAIRVAUX knew a thing or two about monastic life and he once commented that if a monastery didn't have one really annoying person in it, well, it would almost be necessary to introduce one!

"Such a person is a real trial," he wrote, "but learning to deal with them wisely brings astonishing results."

His appreciation doesn't give us a licence to be that challenging person – but it might help us deal a little more kindly with the ones we know!

## Monday — May 15

**I** WONDER if the phrase preceded the John Buchan novel "Mr Standfast", which was published in 1919, or whether it became popular because of the success of that third John Hannay novel.

Hannay, travelling undercover in the Highlands, is asked by Gresson, a man he believes to be a spy, what his agenda for the day is. Hannay outlines a series of hills that has a local man wince. But Gresson grins and says, "It's a great life if you don't weaken."

And he's right! Your tastes might not run to hillwalking but there is a wonderful world – and life – out there if we care to see it.

We risk spoiling both by weakening, but by doing the right thing – being truthful, applying effort, caring for others – we put ourselves in the best possible position to appreciate these words of John Buchan and enjoy what is, indeed, a great life.

## Tuesday — May 16

**A**N old proverb says, "It is hard to count your blessings when sorrow presses so much closer. But though unnumbered, blessings still surround you."

So, when it seems that sorrows and difficulties are surrounding you, say excuse me to these annoying things, push them aside if you must to get a clearer view and then look up to see what really surrounds you!

## Wednesday — May 17

RALPH WALDO EMERSON wrote, "Do not be too timid or squeamish about your actions. All life is an experiment." It seemed a little reckless to me, at first thought. An excuse to be careless and do things people with more sense wouldn't.

But then I thought about the hesitation that often surrounds good things. Like the number of times "I love you" or "You are appreciated" or "Would you like to come round for tea some time?" or other such things go unsaid because people might be embarrassed or worried about the response.

I know a man who was too nervous to hold his father's hand when the older man was ill, just because they had never had that kind of relationship. He wanted to but he didn't know how his father would react, so he didn't.

A lot of good feeling goes unfelt because of our hesitancy. So, if I may paraphrase Mr Emerson a little, when it comes to love and friendship, "Do not be too timid. Experiment!"

## Thursday — May 18

WHEN it comes to running I am good over short distances – like from the front door to the most comfortable spot on the couch. I guess I need to work on my endurance and perseverance.

A BBC report recently told of four Kenyan men who chased two leopards that had been killing local livestock. And they caught them, too.

Then they turned them over to the Kenyan Wildlife Service to be relocated to some other place where they might be less risk. How on earth, you might ask, did they manage that?

Well – they kept on going. A leopard is incredibly fast – but only over short distances. After that initial burst its stamina decreases. By perseverance, over the space of four days, the men pursued the leopards on foot until the creatures just couldn't run any more.

But how does that relate to everyday life? Like this. The next time a problem tries to convince you it is too difficult, ask yourself this: "Is it more difficult than out-running a leopard?" Persevere!

## Friday — May 19

THE movies these days seem full of superheroes with amazing powers. Wouldn't it be nice to have a superpower? Think of the difference it would make to your life! Which would you choose?

Louisa May Alcott, the author of "Little Women", wrote, "The power of finding beauty in the humblest things makes home happy and life lovely."

Now there's a power that really would make a difference to a life. A happy home and a lovely life – and you wouldn't have to fight supervillains!

## Saturday — May 20

THERE'S an old Scots saying – "When we are going up the hill of fortune may we ne'er meet a friend coming down."

Ideally we, and our friends, would travel up the hill together. But surely times of improved fortune are ideal to meet others whose life has taken a downturn, so we can help them back up.

What is the point of climbing the hill in the first place if it's not for the opportunity it gives us to help our friends?

## Sunday — May 21

THE Apostle Matthew tells us that the road to eternal life is narrow and we traditionally think of it as rocky, being full of obstacles and temptations that might encourage us to give up.

The path is, no doubt, longer than the one that runs up Mount Snowdon, but for long stretches, that path is actually made of rocks. Nearby stones have been gathered and pavements and steps built. The hill is still as steep but the way is smoother.

The minister Henry Ward Beecher said, "Every charitable act is a stepping stone toward heaven."

There will undoubtedly be rocks in our path. Whether they are obstacles in our way or a safer surface to travel along may well depend upon how charitable our walk is.

Blue eyes.

## Monday — May 22

*I SAW it in a garden as my bus went dawdling by,*
*A line of wind-tossed washing underneath an azure sky.*
*The breeze was brisk and teasing and it made the branches sway,*
*The washing seemed like bunting hung to welcome in the day,*
*The scarlet socks and tea towels and the trousers, faded blue,*
*The billowed white of bedclothes as they bravely flapped and flew.*
*And then, the bus was moving and the sight was left behind,*
*Yet, visible no longer, still it stayed within my mind,*
*The dancing wind and washing in their jubilant embrace*
*Had blown away my blues and put a smile upon my face.*

– Margaret Ingall.

## Tuesday — May 23

MY neighbour, Bob, has one of those kneeling pads with handles for when he's doing the garden. The pad eases his knees when he's weeding and the handles help him get up again when he's finished.

He told me once he had been reading about the artist and cookbook author Edward Giobbi. Perhaps feeling his aches and pains like Bob, Mr Giobbi wrote, "I think that no matter how old or infirm I may become, I will always plant a large garden in the spring. Who can resist the feelings of hope and joy that one gets from participating in nature's rebirth?"

I know what he meant. And it goes beyond the enjoyment felt by the gardener. It's a feeling shared by everyone who walks past that garden and slows down a little just to gaze in passing.

## Wednesday — May 24

THE Chinese philosopher Confucius is reputed to have said, "Everything has beauty but not everyone sees it."

Everything? I don't know if that can possibly be true but I do know that if I spent the rest of my life testing his theory I would, happily, find more beauty than I could ever have imagined!

## Thursday — May 25

AS far as church goes Michael has no use for preserving false sanctity. If a thing or a place doesn't serve a purpose and if that purpose isn't good for God or man, then it really should go.

Radical words, but perhaps he isn't as radical as he thinks he is.

When his traditional church underwent a renovation he was in there helping tear out the old woodwork, building new walls and splashing on the paint. But when he saw the high-backed chair the minister used to sit on being tossed on to a skip, he just had to rescue it.

As it didn't fit in with his decor or his modernist philosophy I just had to ask him why.

"Oh, I'm not sure," he said, sitting there with his forearms on the leather-covered arm-rests. "I just had an image of the minister preparing his sermons in this chair all those years and I wondered how many thoughts of goodwill and God had been thought in it."

It may not be the soundest theology, but I can't help but think that thoughts of God and goodwill can sanctify many a place, or a piece of furniture, or the person thinking them!

## Friday — May 26

*THE light increases day by day,*
*The sun feels warmer on the skin,*
*Though rain and cloud stand in the way,*
*We feel, we know, that light will win.*
*The leaf-buds open – slowly still –*
*And snowdrops mask the ground, not snow:*
*The gardeners tend their plants with skill,*
*And bulbs begin to dare to grow.*
*The light gives children extra times*
*To chase each other up and down,*
*Along the streets where greening limes*
*Bring life and hope back to the town.*
*The children, they are mankind's spring:*
*And, like the plants, need cherishing.*

– Elizabeth Horrocks.

## Saturday — May 27

LEGEND has it that a king of Ancient Persia sent his three sons on a quest to find the fabled treasure of Serendip.

Many things happened to them on the journey and each difficulty they faced either taught them something, or made them stronger, or helped them along their way. It's where we get the word for a fortuitous happening, serendipity, from.

We might not be princes and princesses, but we are on a journey and how we deal with the things that happen to us will help shape us. Henry David Thoreau meant as much when he wrote, "What you get by achieving your goals is not as important as what you become by achieving your goals."

## Sunday — May 28

MANY and various are the notions as to why we are put on this earth. But I prefer by far the explanation offered by the missionary Henry Drummond.

"Life is not a holiday," he wrote, "but an education! And the one eternal lesson for us all is how better we can love."

## Monday — May 29

BACK in the days when more of us lived off the land there was a saying: "Chop your own wood and you will be twice warmed."

The meaning is pretty obvious. The woodcutter works up a sweat turning the felled tree into firewood. Then, once the wood has been cut and brought into the house, he gets warmed again by the fire.

I am almost compelled to qualify this advice and add a third warmth – the glow that comes from sharing that fire, and the results of your hard work, with family and friends!

Not many of us cut our own firewood these days. But whatever our labours are, be they in the forest, the office or the home, if we put our best into them, enjoy the benefits of them, and share those benefits with others then we, too, will be thrice warmed.

## Tuesday — May 30

I ENJOYED watching a pair of hawks in the field and then my attention was drawn to a noise in the long grass under the trees. A sparrow had become entangled in some fishing line. The sparrow struggled frantically as I picked it up but it soon calmed enough for me to disentangle it and throw it gently into the tree branches where it recovered itself before flying off.

Those beautiful lines by Emily Dickinson came to mind –

"If I can stop one heart from breaking,
I shall not live in vain;
If I can ease one life the aching,
Or cool one pain,
Or help one fainting robin
Unto his nest again,
I shall not live in vain."

Would it surprise you to know that was almost ten years ago and I can still feel that sparrow's heartbeat in the palm of my hand? That day was not spent in vain.

## Wednesday — May 31

A FEW years ago the artist Bruno Catalano unveiled a series of statues in Marseilles called *Les Voyageurs*. The life-sized bronze figures depicted travellers of different sexes and social backgrounds. All of them carried bags.

And through some skilful artistry large parts of each figure, usually from the chest or abdomen, are missing. The statues look like they shouldn't be able to support themselves – but they do. And the Voyagers seem intent on always moving forward.

Could he be saying, I wonder, that the urge to travel is deep in the human psyche, but in travelling we always leave something behind? And can that missing part in every traveller only be filled with home?

For most of us, when we travel, home is the people or place we will always go back to. For some, home is a person or place they hope to find. But, be it behind us or ahead of us, home is always the point of the journey.

And there's nothing to be pessimistic about there!

# June

Thursday — June 1

MAY I, on International Children's Day, share a story with you? Two sisters were asked what they liked about each other.

"She helps me with my sums," the eight-year-old said of the five-year-old. "When I run out of fingers to count on, she lets me use hers."

Now, isn't that just too cute? It is a reminder for me that we are never too young or too small to help, but more than that, it's a reminder of the innocence, the beauty, the hope and potential that children bring into the world. They are to be valued, wherever in the world they are or the political climate they grow up in.

It's no cliché to say that children are our future. How we treat them, encourage them, and teach them they are valued – or not – will end up shaping the world. You can count on that.

Friday — June 2

*THOUGH I've been looking forward to a day of quiet reading,*
*I gaze outside and sigh – I simply can't put off my weeding!*
*They seem so firmly planted, though they've not been growing*
*   long,*
*I only wish my bedding plants and shrubs were half as strong.*
*So out I go, with spade and fork and trusty welly boots*
*Prepared once more to battle with tenacious little roots.*
*I snip off little brambles, do my best to dig them out,*
*Then tug the dandelions from the path in which they sprout.*
*So, tugging, heaving, stretching, reaching, snipping, clipping,*
*   bending,*
*Digging, sweeping – goodness me, this task is never ending!*
*It's difficult to conquer them, but I don't mind a bit.*
*I can't be angry with my weeds – they help to keep me fit!*

*– Emma Canning.*

## Saturday — June 3

DOES power make a person happy? The 19th-century English poet Mary Howitt wrote, "He is happiest who hath power to gather wisdom from a flower."

But the wisdom doesn't come easily, apparently. You need the power to discern it. You might have to visit those flowers for as long as it takes. I never promised that power (or happiness) was easy to get, but I can reassure you that the quest to obtain it can be sweet-smelling and beautiful!

## Sunday — June 4

HENRY WADSWORTH LONGFELLOW described June as, "the fairest daughter of the year." James Russell Lowell wrote, "And what is so rare as a day in June? Then, if ever, come perfect days."

I am reminded of Great-aunt Louisa, who used to go walking in the countryside with books of poetry to see who described those wonders best; the poet or Mother Nature.

"Whoever made the best show on each instance," she wrote, "I was the winner for the simple pleasure of being the judge and the reminder that I was a part of it all."

Perfect days might, or might not, be found in any month of the year. But perfect appreciation is ours to take with us wherever we go.

## Monday — June 5

THE Japanese, it seems, take walks in the woods very seriously. They have a word for the beneficial effects such walks have. *Shinrin-yoku* means "wood air bathing". They also have a word for the sunlight that comes through the leafy canopy; not between the leaves but through them. It's called *komorebi*.

In Britain we might not have such specific terms, but we do like to spend time under the trees, walking, reading or watching the children at play.

Now that I think about it, we do have a word for that. It's "Ahh!"

Summer vitality.

## Tuesday — June 6

ON the anniversary of the D-Day Landings at Normandy I would like to share a few words by the Allied Forces Commander General Eisenhower.

"This operation is not being planned with any alternatives. This operation is planned as a victory, and that's the way it's going to be."

And, of course, he and all the brave men and women of the Allied Forces did indeed achieve that victory.

It also strikes me as not a bad attitude for life!

## Wednesday — June 7

IN L.M. Montgomery's novel "Anne Of Green Gables", Anne wonders "What it would be like to live in a world where it was always June."

Well, June will come and go, as it should, but that doesn't mean we can't keep the warmth, the vitality, the colour and all the other things that make it such a special month alive in our personality and how we interact with the world throughout every other month of the year.

## Thursday — June 8

JACK ANTHONY may be a name from the past or he may still be among us – he may be a venerable old man of letters or a teenager posting on his blog. So, what do I know about him? I know he has an important reminder to share on the importance of appreciation.

"I have never been a millionaire," he wrote, "but I have enjoyed a great meal, a crackling fire, a glorious sunset, a walk with a friend, a hug from a child, a cup of soup, a kiss behind the ear. There are plenty of life's tiny delights for all of us."

Every one of those delights is free – and wonderful! We don't need to be millionaires to abundantly enjoy this world and this life.

"Plenty"? There's more than that. And the more you look the more there are!

## Friday — June 9

HOW many times have someone else's actions left you not knowing whether to laugh or cry?

The Dutch philosopher Baruch Spinoza, who lived in the 17th century and is generally regarded as one of Europe's greatest thinkers, chose a different way.

"I have taken great care not to laugh at human actions," he wrote, "nor to weep at them, nor to hate them, but to understand them."

Understanding is, of course, the more difficult path to walk but laughter and tears are over in moments, hate is never a positive option, which just leaves understanding. It may never be achieved this side of heaven, but in the attempt we may also come to understand ourselves a little better.

## Saturday — June 10

THE historian Thomas Andrew Bailey once strayed a little from his main subject and wrote, "There must surely be such a thing as a child of average abilities, but you can't find a parent who will admit it's their child."

Every parent thinks their child is special and I'm sure God thinks the same about all of us – even the worst of us. Only . . . He's more likely to be right!

## Sunday — June 11

HE was a theologian, an organist, a philosopher, a physician and a medical missionary. You wouldn't be wrong if you guessed that Albert Schweitzer knew a lot of stuff!

But, even after all his schooling and training was done, there were four things he still wanted to learn; things we might all benefit from learning.

They were – "To think clearly without hurry or confusion, to love everybody sincerely, to act in everything with the highest motives, and to trust in God unhesitatingly."

## Monday — June 12

L EFT-OVERS can often make some pretty delicious meals.
Ask any mum who has ever made cookies or cakes with the "help"
of children and they will tell you that the mix or the chocolate left in
the bowl often seems to be more delicious than the finished product.

Hark back to the story of Ruth in the Bible and you remember she
was allowed to feed herself and her mother-in-law from the crops
left in the fields after the harvest had been taken in.

It was seen as a requirement of their faith that those blessed
enough to have fields and crops owed it to God or society to leave
something for others.

Left-overs seem to have some pretty wonderful qualities. We are
blessed indeed if we live a life that fills our needs and then some. So,
let us not neglect those extras and endeavour to put them to good
use. You never know . . . the more you see the magic worked by
left-overs, the more you might want to leave!

## Tuesday — June 13

D O you know any cynics? Perhaps you do – but they might not be
the people you think they are.

Cynicism was originally an Ancient Greek school of thought in
which people lived the simplest of lives possible. Possessions, power,
ambition and other material aspects of life were seen as distractions
from a pure life.

One of its most famous adherents was Diogenes of Sinope who
had no home and few possessions.

Once, while sleeping in a large ceramic tub in an Athenian
market-place, he was visited by Alexander the Great. Alexander
asked if there was anything he could do for the famous Cynic.

Diogenes replied, "You could step to one side and give me back
the gift of the sunshine."

Now, I'm not recommending sleeping in tubs, but perhaps there's
a lesson there somewhere when it comes to simplifying our lives.
Maybe we could all do with a little more real cynicism in our lives.

## Wednesday — June 14

IN the Book of Matthew Jesus says, "Man does not live on bread alone but on every word from the mouth of God."

John Muir would have agreed and he knew some wonderful places to listen for those words. A Scottish naturalist in America in the 19th century, he helped areas like Yosemite achieve National Park status.

Muir once wrote, "Everybody needs beauty as well as bread, places to play in and pray in, where nature may heal and give strength to body and soul."

I'm not suggesting we go off exploring a vast wilderness like Muir did, but we might follow his advice and find a place to play and pray. Especially for those times when the "bread" of the material world isn't enough to satisfy you.

## Thursday — June 15

JOHN GUNTHER was famous for the amount of research he put into his books. So, when we hear he had something to say about happiness, we can be assured he researched the subject thoroughly.

Late in his life he offered the considered opinion that, "All happiness depends on a leisurely breakfast."

It's a theory I think should be tested for at least as long as it took Mr Gunther to come up with it. Don't you?

## Friday — June 16

WHAT is it that makes life so special? That's a deep question we could spend many a week or month or year debating!

The clergyman and poet Henry van Dyke had a simpler take on it.

"Be glad of life," he wrote, "because it gives you the chance to love and to work and to play and to look up at the stars."

"Really, Henry?" we might ask. "Is that all?"

But imagine if we could never again do any one of those things. How much we would miss! It is, after all, the so-called simple things that make this life so wonderful.

Verdant view.

## Saturday — June 17

ROBERT B. THOMAS was the son of a Welsh man who worked on "The Old Farmer's Almanac", which informed country folk about tides, phases of the moon, planting times, etc. It mixes those facts with interesting articles, jokes and words of wisdom.

That mix might well sum up the philosophy of Robert B. Thomas. "Strive always to be useful," he told his readership, "but with a pleasant degree of humor."

We can be useful without being pleasant, but a smile and a kind word seem to multiply the usefulness of the one who shares them – in every phase of the moon!

## Sunday — June 18

A YOUNG woman in the United States came up with the idea of Father's Day. Sonora Smart wanted to honour her dad, William, a Civil War veteran who raised six children on his own.

In Spain Father's Day is celebrated on the feast day of Saint Joseph, the earthly father of Jesus. In Thailand it's a movable feast celebrated on the birthday of the current king. In China it is celebrated on the eighth day of the eighth month. The Chinese for eight is "ba" and "ba-ba" sounds quite like their word for daddy.

So, this Father's Day, let's give thanks for our dads, but take a moment to give thanks to "Our Father" for all His love and care. He is, after all, the standard good fathers aspire to!

## Monday — June 19

IS it always desirable to be learned? Can there be greater joy in simplicity?

Bertrand Russell once wrote, "Every time I talk to a savant (or learned person) I feel quite sure that happiness is no longer a possibility. Yet when I talk with my gardener, I am convinced of the opposite."

Perhaps it is that happiness is to be found in something that requires our attention and effort to help it along but where the results and the real responsibilities are ultimately in the hands of God.

## Tuesday — June 20

PRAYER can be a difficult subject to tackle. Do we pray to God to change our situation when we believe Him to be in control of our situation? Do we pray for things or further blessing while believing that "the Lord will provide."?

There's a story of a father who hears his little daughter repeating the alphabet the best she can. But he notices she has her eyes closed. He asks her what she's doing and she opens one eye to look at him.

"I'm praying, Daddy," she whispers.

"It sounded an awful lot like your letters," he said.

"Mummy says letters make up all the words," his daughter explained, "and sometimes when I pray to God I don't know what I want to say, so I give Him all the letters and let Him turn them into the right words."

There is great truth in this. Even as adults it can be difficult to find the right words, so perhaps we ought to borrow that little girl's faith and hand it all over to God.

Maybe the only prayer we need is trust.

## Wednesday — June 21

HAVE you heard of "the empty fort strategy"? It comes from a Chinese legend but can be usefully applied to each of our lives.

A governor was tasked with defending a city against an oncoming army. The only problem was that the enemy had a hundred times the soldiers he had. He could have barricaded his people in for a long siege, but instead he sent his army away.

When the enemy arrived they found the city defenceless, the gates open and the governor sitting by a fountain with his children. They were playing with paper boats.

The commander of the enemy army was thoroughly confused. This was like nothing he had ever experienced, so his mind told him it must be a trap and he ordered a full-scale retreat!

Sometimes we can surprise our everyday fears by saying, "OK, here I am. Do your worst." That's when we are likely to discover that our fears aren't so fearsome after all.

## Thursday — June 22

IT'S all too easy to get carried away with our expectation of how life should be; with what we think we have earned or deserve. Of course, life has a way of thwarting even the most reasonable plans and bitterness is often the result.

In his Choruses from "The Rock", the poet T.S. Eliot advised mankind to "take no thought of the harvest but only of proper sowing."

In other words, do what you do the best way you can, trust in God – and wait to see what grows!

## Friday — June 23

*IN the garden of the heart*
*Grow seeds of love and trust;*
*Where honesty proliferates,*
*Where all is kind and just.*
*A garden warm and comforting,*
*Welcoming and splendid,*
*Where those who gladly step inside*
*Are nurtured and defended.*

*– Emma Canning.*

## Saturday — June 24

THE musician Herbie Hancock recalled a time in his youth when he was invited to play with the legendary Miles Davis. Can you imagine? The novice playing with the master!

It all went well until Hancock played a wrong chord. He cringed with embarrassment, disappointed in himself, and fully expecting Davis to stop and berate him.

But Davis's response was one we might all learn from. He kept on playing and, as Hancock explained, "He played some notes that made my wrong chord right."

## Sunday — June 25

WE read in the Bible of Cain's guilty, defensive challenge to God after he killed Abel. "Am I my brother's keeper?" he demanded to know.

The blues legend B.B. King had another point of view. "I can't think of anyone I have mistreated," he said. "I have always thought I am my brother's keeper."

When it comes to our brothers and sisters in the bigger, human family we are all allowed to ask the question. The answer we give will define the world we live in.

## Monday — June 26

AGED thirty-eight, he was appointed choirmaster of a church, but only on condition he also taught Latin. He was the third choice for the position and only got the job because two others turned it down. When he asked for a pay rise some time later he was told he was free to find a better wage elsewhere.

If ever you are feeling under-appreciated then hum yourself a little of his Suite Number 3 (known to a certain generation as the theme from the Hamlet cigar advert) and tell yourself the world eventually recognised Johann Sebastian Bach as one of the greatest composers ever. It will recognise you eventually.

## Tuesday — June 27

HOME is the place where, when you have to go there, they have to take you in" comes from the Robert Frost poem "The Death Of The Hired Man". But the following lines read – "I should have called it /Something you somehow haven't to deserve."

Home – something you somehow haven't to deserve. How many of us, looking back on our childhood antics, are glad we didn't have to deserve the loving home we grew up in?

There's something almost heavenly about the idea. Which, given that Heaven is our ultimate home, is really rather wonderfully fitting.

## Wednesday — June 28

*TROUBLES may be lessened with someone at your side,*
*Someone who can help you, in whom you can confide.*
*Sharing others' problems soon fades a worried frown;*
*Brings relief from fretting when life has let you down.*
*Let's all help our neighbours with kindly words to say,*
*For those now feeling lonely, it's sure to make their day.*
*We should make the effort and be the ones to lead –*
*What a worthwhile comfort to be a friend in need!*

– Elizabeth Gozney.

## Thursday — June 29

WHAT does God want of us is a big question! The prophet Micah answered it like this – "Act justly and to love mercy and to walk humbly with your God."

A commentary in the Talmud brings it into perspective. "Do not be daunted by the enormity of the world's grief. Do justly now. Love mercy now. Walk humbly now. You are not obligated to complete the work but neither are you free to abandon it."

Do what you can now. And remember, it is always now.

## Friday — June 30

THE ornamental gardens were beautiful – but not to be touched. There was, however, another section called the Gateway to Childhood.

Here were streams to be walked in, boats to float, caves to run through, and chimes and bells to be played.

As there must be these days, there was a set of rules just inside the gate. *Be Curious, Be Safe, Be Respectful. But most of all, be curious.*

Time and again we are encouraged to learn from children, so perhaps I can suggest that the rules good enough for Childhood's Gateway might also be worth following for the rest of our lives.

Be safe, be respectful, and always be curious!

# July

## Saturday — July 1

U NLESS you are in Hollywood, footprints in cement are usually accidental and quickly smoothed away. But I know of two instances where they were left. And they were made at either end of life.

Jean's dad was a Pathfinder in the RAF during World War II. He and his fellow pilots flew into occupied Europe ahead of any ground attack.

In later life he all but lost his sight, and wandered on to some wet cement. Two shallow prints remain and Jean often stands in them, remembering the man who set her on her path through life.

The other, smaller, step is in front of a church. Some time ago a weary mother stood her toddler down on a step that was being repaired and hadn't set yet.

I hear that when the labourer went to wipe the marks away the gaffer told him, "Stay your hand, lad. The Lord surely won't mind a child's footprints leading the way into His house."

## Sunday — July 2

H AVE you ever had one of those days when it seems the whole world is out to get you?"

Our dear friend Mary knew I was only having a grumble. But she put her shopping down and put her serious face on.

"That's called paranoia," she said, "and there are all kinds of treatments for it. I suffer from the opposite problem."

I knew I was being led along a path but Mary's meanderings are always such pretty places to go, so I asked, "And what is that?"

"Pronoia," she told me, "the belief that the universe is actually out to help you. It's a condition for which there is no cure."

I don't know about the whole universe, but Mary certainly seems put here to help me. And the least I can do in return is share her "condition" with as many others as I can.

## Monday — July 3

CHARLES and Emmie are just back from a holiday in Colorado. While they were there they visited the Garden of the Gods. It's a National Natural Landmark.

The red rock makes it look like the surface of Mars might. We spent a happy afternoon oohing and aahing at the photos, and we all agreed it had been a once in a lifetime experience for them both.

That evening I went out in a fine mist; the grass around me was tall and lush, buttercups were everywhere . . . In the stillness I gave thanks that the garden of God is all around us and no less wonderful for being so commonplace.

## Tuesday — July 4

JAMES is a mountaineer and hill-walker of long experience. Give him a map and a compass and he can find any location to within a few feet, but he once told me he had a terrible sense of direction.

"How can that be?" I asked.

"Well," he replied, "I often forget which way is forwards."

His point was, it doesn't matter so much whether you go east, west, north or south. What matters is that your journey moves you (and possibly others) on!

## Wednesday — July 5

SOME anonymous wit once said, "When you are born you look like your mother and father. As you get older you start to look more and more like the decisions you made!"

There's no doubt the decisions we make shape our lives, but do they also affect our appearance? The pursuit of beauty can be an expensive business. Imagine if there was a cheaper way – like being kind, generous and loving!

It might make a difference or it might not. But I guarantee it would make a difference to the appearances of the people you meet along the way – when you leave them with smiles on their faces!

God's beautiful garden is all around us.

## Thursday — July 6

A COLLEGE professor told the graduating class their lives in the future could be seen as vases – empty and dusty, or full of the collected flowers of beauty and kindness. The mum of one of the graduates was dismayed when her son suggested that her "vase" would be empty.

Thankfully, the new graduate didn't stop there.

"Whenever you find a flower of beauty or kindness," he said, "you pass it on to someone else."

I think the student may have understood more about beauty and kindness than his professor did.

## Friday — July 7

HAVE you ever experienced the full force of a two-year-old's curiosity? They reach a certain point and then every second thing they say is, "Why?"

The Greek philosopher Socrates would have understood the "why years" very well. He said, "Wonder is the beginning of wisdom."

Two-year-olds have everything to learn but those of us of more mature years shouldn't try to pretend that we know it all. The world is still full of miracles, mysteries and endlessly renewing beauty. Let's get back in touch with our inner toddler and always be wise enough to wonder, no matter what age we are.

Just don't ask me why!

## Saturday — July 8

THE poet Oliver Goldsmith wasn't alone in liking old stuff. "I love everything that is old," he wrote, "old friends, old times, old manners, old books, old wines."

But if we would lose ourselves in those delights, we must also pay our respects to the new – which those old things once were. The best of them will stay the course and one day be old, to be enjoyed by the generations to come.

## Sunday — July 9

IT was a maxim of the great 20th-century photographer Ansel Adams that there were always at least two people in every picture: the photographer and the viewer.

It occurred to me that we might play a similar role in every encounter we have with another.

Go into each encounter with such an attitude that if a photo was taken there and then of the other person you would be in it, too – in their posture, in their smile, in the happiness in their eyes looking back at you.

## Monday — July 10

WATCHING the tennis at Wimbledon, I am reminded that there is an important distinction between amateurs and professionals in the world of sport. But I doubt that distinction exists in the hearts of the players.

Why? Well, the professionals wouldn't achieve that status without a lot of dedicated effort. Where does that dedication come from? Usually from a love of their game.

And what's the Latin word for someone who loves what they do? *Amator* – from which we get the word amateur.

So, if you have an interest, a sport, a hobby, a passion, and you want to make the most of it, be professional and practise like an amateur!

## Tuesday — July 11

SINCE Adam and Eve were driven out of paradise no-one has ever rediscovered the Garden of Eden. Perhaps it simply doesn't exist on earth any more or perhaps, as the poet Emily Dickinson suggests, it took on a new form and we have been finding it without realising it ever since. She wrote –

"Eden is that old-fashioned house we dwell in every day,
Without suspecting our abode until we drive away."

## Wednesday — July 12

PERHAPS in his younger days he had been a punk. He probably had a whole list of things he was against. Getting an "anarchy" tattoo on the side of his neck probably seemed like a good thing back then. But now he was sitting next to me at a school music show, applauding proudly as his daughter finished her violin solo.

Most of us – as individuals or as societies – will go through a rebellious phase. The artist Van Gogh described the way out.

"But in the end," he wrote, "we shall have had enough of cynicism, scepticism and humbug, and we shall want to live more musically."

My neighbour at the show certainly seemed to want to. May we – as individuals and as a society – learn to do the same.

## Thursday — July 13

FRIENDS can be defined in a multitude of ways. Who first came up with this one I don't know, but it is certainly worth sharing.

"A friend is one who looks over our broken fence to admire the flowers in our garden."

The broken fence in our lives might be a physical or emotional restriction of some sort, it might be a difference in our priorities, but there will always be something in our lives worth admiring.

A friend is the one who looks over our limitations – our broken fences – and finds the beauty blooming within them.

## Friday — July 14

BENNY had been talking to a man who credited him with saving his life a while back. He said, "It was the worst time of my life – and then God sent an angel to save me." He thought about it, and added, "Of course, you weren't my first idea of an angel."

We both laughed at that. Benny is six feet tall, carries some extra weight, is bald and usually dresses quite scruffily.

Angels may come in many guises, but it is always their heart that defines them.

Berry nice!

## Saturday — July 15

EVERY year around this time the city of Pamplona in Spain hosts the San Fermin Festival, which includes the tradition of running with the bulls. After over a week of revelry, the ceremony comes to a close with the mass singing of *Pobre Di Mi* – Poor Me – and is about how sad it is that the festival is over.

The sad song is sung joyfully by people linking arms or waving candles; there are speeches and people dressed up in bull costumes.

All things come to an end, but the closing ceremony of San Fermin reminds us that endings can be wonderful as well, anticipating as they do the next time, or leaving the way open for something new.

## Sunday — July 16

ON holiday in Japan Mary was fascinated by the torii gates she saw there. Constructed from two camphor wood pillars and a decorated lintel, they often sit outside Buddhist or Shinto temples and mark the transition from the profane to the sacred.

But many stood in patches of ground with no connection to a temple and no way to know which way was "out" and which was "in."

"In a way that probably wasn't intended," Mary told me, "it reminded me that no part of God's Creation is profane. It's all sacred."

## Monday — July 17

THE other day I spent a few minutes watching a butterfly in a hawthorn hedge. What it was doing fluttering among the tightly twisted branches, I don't know. I was just amazed that it managed it without ripping a wing on one of the many thorns surrounding it.

Perhaps the butterfly doesn't have to flap its wings with any great force to stay aloft. Perhaps the trick is in flapping so gently that when wing and thorn do come into contact the one slides so gently over the other that no damage is done.

Now, if only we could take ourselves that lightly. Think where we might walk without causing or receiving any wounds.

## Tuesday — July 18

READING about the life of the composer J.S. Bach, one of his lesser-known performances captured my imagination.

His reputation today is of a great composer, but his fame was hard-earned. One day he turned up at a church to debut a new composition – and no-one appeared to hear it!

What did Bach do? He told the musicians they were going to play anyway. God would hear them. And I have no doubt that, in a way they never expected to, they all thoroughly enjoyed the performance.

The question the great composer must have asked himself is as relevant today as it was then. Am I doing this for the acclaim of the public, or because I love it and my heart and soul are in it?

If it's the former, we will set ourselves up for disappointment. If it's the latter, then we will make beautiful music no matter what we do.

## Wednesday — July 19

THE shredder in Martin's office gets plenty of use disposing of confidential documents. But that isn't its primary use.

You see, Martin has a mail policy that forbids him sending out letters written in anger until at least twenty-four hours later. Then he reads them again.

Usually, they are returned to the drawer he reserves for such letters. He feels better for having written them, getting all that frustration out his system, and he feels better still for not having upset anyone or damaged any relationships by sending them. And once a month the shredder gets a good workout disposing of the evidence.

It's a technique that could surely be used to good effect in everyday life. Write those angry retorts down, getting them out of your head, and go back to them the next day.

And if I may add a little something to Martin's philosophy . . . treat yourself to something nice. You already made the world a sweeter place for not shredding someone with your angry words, so you deserve it!

## Thursday — July 20

*I'M just an armchair traveller, I don't go far from home.*
*My passport's long expired,*
*Though once I loved to roam.*
*But, still, I'm not complaining,*
*You'll see no sign of gloom*
*With so much all around me*
*To help my interest bloom.*
*I've books and films and photos*
*Of strange and wondrous sights,*
*Of ocean deeps, and deserts,*
*Hot skies and northern lights.*
*I shan't give up my hobby with such marvels still to see;*
*I may no longer roam the world – instead, it comes to me!*

– Margaret Ingall.

## Friday — July 21

HOW we recover from a setback says a lot about us as people and as a people. Take the church of St Ethelburga in London. Built in the 1400s, it survived the Great Fire and the Blitz. But in 1993 it was almost completely destroyed by an IRA bomb.

The end of the story? No. St Ethelburga's Church was rebuilt as St Ethelburga's Centre for reconciliation and peace.

When someone knocks you down the best response is to take the chance while you are down there to help someone else up!

## Saturday — July 22

A SHEPHERD all through his long working life, Les occasionally spent nights on the hills tending expectant ewes. There usually wasn't much to do except hunker down and wait for the morning. Les would spend time with his thoughts, then he would tell them to "wheesht while the Lord does the talking."

I doubt if many of us will be in that situation, but most of us could probably find a time each day that would otherwise be given over to frustration, and "wheesht" while another Shepherd talks.

## Sunday — July 23

IF you look closely enough in the middle of summer you can see the beginnings of autumn. Those brambles and horse chestnuts don't just appear from nowhere, you know. The preparatory work begins about halfway through the previous season.

Another way of looking at it is that each season is its own wonderful self but is also the servant of the season to come.

It wouldn't be a bad way to live our lives either: exploring how wonderful this world is, but spending just as much time being the servant of the world to come.

## Monday — July 24

PEOPLE often extoll the benefits of a good walk or, in some way, getting out and about in the natural world. One of the greatest musicians who ever lived credited the activity as a major influence on his work.

"How happy I am," Beethoven wrote, "to be able to walk among the shrubs, the trees, the woods, the grass and the rocks! For the woods, the trees and the rocks give man the resonance he needs."

If you can get out and about I am sure you will understand what the great composer meant. If you can't, then his beautiful music, inspired by those walks, will surely have a similarly uplifting effect.

## Tuesday — July 25

MARGARET was putting together a choir for a competition. "I have had to turn away some beautiful singers," she told me. "I'm at the point where I don't need exceptional voices, I need voices that work well with the ones we already have in the choir."

There was a lesson in there, I was sure. It was this – there will always be a place (and rich rewards) for the outstanding talents, but sometimes what we need is simply people who will complement each other and work well together. As Margaret was finding out, that can be as rare (and as valuable) a talent as any other.

## Wednesday — July 26

WHAT is an oasis? It is nothing more than the place, in a dry area, where water reaches the surface. And yet, that water makes such a difference!

I don't believe I have ever visited one of those – but I have been blessed to encounter several of another kind.

The American essayist Washington Irving described my favourite sort of oasis like this – "A kind heart is a fountain of gladness making everything in its vicinity freshen into smiles."

Whichever type of an oasis it might be, it seems they still make all the difference!

## Thursday — July 27

THE sign on the bookshop shelf read –"If you can't see the book you want – write it yourself!"

I am sure it was meant for a laugh and didn't reflect their level of customer service, but it did remind me that every book you might like to read, every painting you love, every film you like to watch, was made by someone just like you who set out to do that thing.

That's not to say it's easy, but it can always be done.

So, if you find your bookshelves, or your life, is missing something then you can actually fill that space. And then maybe you can write a best-selling book about how you did it!

## Friday — July 28

TO live is like love," Samuel Butler wrote. "All reason is against it, and all healthy instinct for it."

The most precious things in life so often make little practical sense. Why should we look twice at beauty? Why should we help another at expense to ourself?

In a world run on survival-of-the-fittest guidelines, these things would be seen as unreasonable or contrary to survival. But we instinctively do them. And the more we do them the more wonderful and beautiful "survival" becomes.

## Saturday — July 29

THEY say all the water in the world can't sink a ship – unless it gets inside! Likewise, the negative aspects of life can't bring us down unless we let them in.

Walking through a wood in the Lake District, I came to a place where new trees had been planted. Now deer like nothing better than to nibble on saplings. And they can jump! So the people working the forest put an eight-foot-tall fence around that area.

But rabbits, hedgehogs and other little creatures also use the woods and are no threat to the saplings. So little foot-high by foot-wide doorways were spaced along the bottom of the fence.

It took a bit of work but the negative stayed out and the positive came in.

## Sunday — July 30

THERE'S a story of a missionary who was about to retire. One man, who lived three days' walk away, presented him with a wooden carving he had made specially.

The missionary said, "Brother, I can't believe you walked so far to bring this to me." The man clasped his hand and replied, "The walk is part of the gift."

Every gift we give or receive will have more to it than its face value. Look beyond the gift to the time, effort, love and consideration it took to bring it to you – and put something of yourself into every gift you give.

## Monday — July 31

KATHY and Gwen have been friends from schooldays, since when many other things have come and gone from their lives, but their friendship is still going strong.

Dorothy Parker could have been referring to them when she wrote, "Constant use has not worn ragged the fabric of their friendship."

Indeed, constant use makes friendship grow stronger and last longer!

# August

## Tuesday — August 1

**B**ERNARD and Caroline are missionaries in Chad, which sits near the centre of the African continent. The country's official language is French and English is the language used for work.

Not having a word of French when they moved there, our friends took steps to learn as quickly as they could. But the biggest step forward in their work, the biggest improvement in their relations with their neighbours, and also the thing that brought the biggest smiles, was when they learned to speak the local version of Arabic. It was the language the population had largely grown up with and not a remnant from colonial times, or something brought in from elsewhere.

As Caroline put it, "It's the language of their heart."

How better, I wondered, to communicate your faith or anything else than by speaking to people in the language of their heart?

## Wednesday — August 2

**H**AVE you ever wondered why tightrope walkers carry a pole?

The best I can come up with is that, if you're holding it tightly, it's difficult to topple to the left because there is so much weight out there on the right. And difficult to topple to the right because there is so much weight out there on the left.

Of course, the difficult job of walking the wire remains, but the pole helps keep the walker upright.

If only we had something like that for the less adventurous of us. But, of course, we do. The inspirational writer William Arthur Ward pointed it out.

"A well-developed sense of humor is the pole that adds balance to your steps as you walk the tightrope of life."

Just don't laugh too enthusiastically!

Playtime!

## Thursday — August 3

WATCHING a recent film of "Cinderella", I was struck by two things. The first was that, despite everything, Cinderella was happier than her stepsisters who had their every whim catered to.

The second thing was that glass slippers, no matter how beautiful they look, must be awfully uncomfortable!

Two thoughts which came together nicely in words of wisdom by John Bunyan. The author of "The Pilgrim's Progress" wrote, "If we have not quiet in our minds outward comfort will do no more for us than a golden slipper on a gouty foot."

Find the contentment of love and you shall, indeed, go to the ball, because the whole world will seem like a ball!

## Friday — August 4

A FLOWER-ARRANGER shared this thought with me. Anyone who has ever attempted that art will understand.

"Children," she said, "are like the flowers in an arrangement. There's always one determined to face the wrong way no matter how carefully you place them."

Of course it's not only children who are like that. The streak of individuality runs through many an adult as well. But the flower is no less true to itself, and no less beautiful, because it doesn't do what all the other flowers do.

## Saturday — August 5

DO you ever feel old? What if I were to suggest you were new instead?

Let's face it, unless you spent the last 24 hours asleep you know more now than you did then, and your store of experiences is larger now than it was then. The person you are today has never existed before. That can be a wonderful thing!

It's an insight I enjoy more and more as time passes, but I can't claim it as mine. It was the poet Emily Dickinson who wrote, "We turn not older with the years, but newer every day."

## Sunday — August 6

IN one of her letters from a bygone era, Great-aunt Louisa talked about the tradition of setting an extra place at the dinner table for Jesus.

It wasn't a tradition Louisa's mother indulged in. She had a difficult enough time feeding her family.

But every Sunday the family was joined by Mrs Biggar, a widow with less to survive on than most. So Louisa's mother made sure that when they had meat to eat Mrs Biggar dined with them.

"An empty seat at the dinner table in remembrance of the Lord is a beautiful thing," Great-aunt Louisa wrote, "but a seat filled by one in need in His name is glorious."

## Monday — August 7

IT was E.B. White, the author of the children's classic "Charlotte's Web", who wrote, "Always be on the lookout for the presence of wonder."

This is a world of seemingly infinite variety and there will be much in the day to see that is wonderful.

Charlotte the spider was in the habit of writing words for Wilbur the pig in her webbing. One of those words was "splendid". If we could live as E.B. White recommended, seeing wonders wherever we go, well, that really would be splendid!

## Tuesday — August 8

IMAGINE spending all your time looking after yourself! In general I wouldn't recommend the approach, but Benjamin Franklin, a much wiser man than I, had a different take on the situation.

"When you are good to others," he wrote, "you are best to yourself."

It's against all expectations, but often putting other people first can be the best thing you do for yourself. So, go on, treat yourself to some kindness directed at others today. You will feel better for it!

## Wednesday — August 9

THESE days, especially as you get older, there seem to be more health checks, which is undoubtedly a good thing.

But how do we measure the health of those more indefinable aspects of us? Ralph Waldo Emerson, the essayist and poet, came up with a good test for our personalities as long ago as the mid-19th century.

"An individual has a healthy personality," he wrote, "to the exact degree to which they have the propensity to look for the good in every situation."

It may not be an exact method, it may not yield measurable results, but it has stood the test of time and it will do for me.

## Thursday — August 10

I LIKE the story of the boss of a big company who sent an e-mail out to his employees. To show how important he thought each of them was he typed the entire message without using the letter "e". It made no sense until he rewrote it with that missing letter included.

"Nobody notices the letter 'e' normally," he wrote, "and you might feel nobody notices the work you do. But we'd be in big trouble without you."

Whether you feel it or not, you make a difference and the world would make a lot less sense without you.

## Friday — August 11

BACK in 1628 the heavily armed Swedish warship *Vasa* set out from Stockholm. King Gustavus Adolphus meant her to be a symbol of his power. Her maiden voyage lasted all of 1400 yards, then her own weight pulled her under the sea.

In contrast, I offer these words of wisdom by G.K. Chesterton – "Angels can fly because they take themselves lightly."

It's a choice we make in our lives: be pulled down by the weight of worldly things, or take ourselves more lightly and soar on the wings of love.

## Saturday — August 12

WINSTON CHURCHILL, perhaps the greatest Prime Minister the country ever had, was definitely a success.

But, of course, the measure of someone is how they cope when things aren't going their way. And Churchill knew plenty of those times as well.

"Success," Churchill said, "is stumbling from failure to failure with no loss of enthusiasm."

That enthusiasm in the face of repeated setbacks is what gets you there in the end and it might, as well as anything, define the British spirit that Churchill came to symbolise.

## Sunday — August 13

HARRY is just back from a holiday in Kazan in Russia. He particularly wanted to show me their "Palace of Agriculture".

It's an impressively ornate building, constructed in a traditional still but made more useable by some impressive modern alterations. And there's a tree in the doorway! Actually, the doorway is a sixty-feet-tall arch and the towering oak that seems to fill it is a piece of art.

"Well," Harry pointed out, "if we can't be reminded that life on this planet is about man-made things and nature in a Palace of Agriculture then where can we?"

## Monday — August 14

HORATIUS BONAR was a prolific writer, preacher and hymnwriter. His would have been a "weel kent" name in the 19th century.

"Let my name lie unknown," he wrote. "It is not the memory of me that should pass on through the ages but the truth of which I have spoken and the things for which I have lived."

He didn't get his way. The name of this good man lives on in hymn books and history books. He is remembered, but the request started me thinking! Is there a greater way to contentment than to find something that is greater than yourself – and to live for it?

## Tuesday — August 15

MUCH has been written about the pursuit of happiness and most people believe it to be good thing. Lloyd Douglas, who wrote the novel "The Robe", had a different idea.

"It was probably a mistake to pursue happiness," he wrote. "Much better to create happiness; still better to create happiness for others. The more happiness you created for others the more would be yours – a solid satisfaction that no-one could ever take away from you."

When you chase something there's always a chance it will get away. Instead, stay where you are and build it!

## Wednesday — August 16

SAMUEL BUTLER, the Victorian novelist and translator, wasn't a man for saying, "I can't." But neither was he a man for making great claims as to his ability.

"If we attend continually and promptly to the little that we can do," he wrote, "we shall ere long be surprised to find how little remains that we cannot do."

Someone else once put the same thought into more "casual" language.

"Yard by yard, life's awful hard. Inch by inch, it's a cinch."

## Thursday — August 17

HENRY THOREAU and Ralph Waldo Emerson were two of the greatest intellects of recent centuries. And they were friends. So, what happens when you put two great thinkers together like that?

Well, Thoreau once stated that the key to living well was to "simplify, simplify, simplify." With a straight face Emerson pointed out that, "One simplify might have sufficed."

It seems that a great intellect can still include a sense of humour. Emerson also said that, "It's one of the blessings of old friends that you can afford to be stupid with them."

So, even smart people like to take some time off!

A S I walked through the wood on a bright, sunny day,
I was dwarfed by the trees that were lining my way,
I was choosing my path and avoiding tree roots
As they all seemed determined to ambush my boots.

With the feel of the breeze in the small, open glade
And the dank smell of bracken in sun-dappled shade,
A small rabbit caught sight of me trudging on by
And was suddenly gone in the wink of an eye.

I saw squirrels cavorting with consummate ease
While birds chirped and cawed in the tops of the trees.
I was filled with delight at each sight, smell and sound.
They were all just for me, with no others around.

Near the edge of the wood, it was both dark and bright,
Where the trees broke the ways of the low-angled light.
I came to a stile where I stopped, and just stood;
And I savoured the joy of that walk in the wood.

– Dennis W. Turner.

## Saturday — August 19

H AVE you ever fallen out with anyone?

I'm guessing here – based on personal experience – that there were probably many good things about your friendship. And one less nice thing that broke it.

Joseph Addison, the co-founder of "The Spectator", wrote, "If men would consider not so much wherein they differ, as wherein they agree, there would be far less of uncharitableness and angry feeling in the world."

Now, back to that person you fell out with.

Not that I'm asking you to think again, but how many things came between you? And how many did you enjoy together?

Really upcycling!

112

## Sunday — August 20

MANY stories have been told about "Woodbine Willie" who preached in the trenches during World War I. My favourite involves a group of soldiers setting up barbed-wire fences in No-man's Land. They were surprised to find the pastor crawling towards them.

"Who are you?" one of the Tommies asked.

"The church," came the reply.

"What's the church doing out here?" someone asked.

"Its job!" Woodbine Willie informed them.

A reminder that sometimes we have to put ourselves "out there" to reach the people God needs reaching.

## Monday — August 21

MAKING up with a friend after harsh words have been exchanged is one of life's more difficult challenges, but the New Zealand-born writer Katherine Mansfield seemed to get it just right.

She wrote, "I am treating you as my friend, asking you to share my present minuses in the hope I can ask you to share my future pluses."

An attitude that is bound to turn the present minus of a lost friendship into the future plus of a happy ever after!

Now, those are the kind of sums I enjoy!

## Tuesday — August 22

*LET us join in celebration for the beauty of each day,*
*Nature fading, yet renewing, life which never goes away,*
*Seasons turning, seasons passing, shining summer, golden fall,*
*New life waking in the springtime, winter simply cradles all.*
*Glory on the moors and hilltops, fragrance on the dew-kissed grass,*
*Stars and oceans live for ever, only time itself will pass.*
*Let us join in celebration of the earth that round us lies,*
*Nature's promise of tomorrow and the life that never dies.*

– Iris Hesselden.

## Wednesday — August 23

FAILURE! Is there any point in talking about it? The pastor and motivational speaker Robert Schuller had several takes on the theme. They included:

Failure doesn't mean you are a failure; it does mean you haven't succeeded yet.

Failure doesn't mean you have accomplished nothing; it does mean you have learned something.

Failure doesn't mean you have been disgraced; it does mean you were willing to try.

And most importantly: Failure doesn't mean God has abandoned you – it does mean God has a better idea!

## Thursday — August 24

A LINE by the poet William Bryant caught my attention. It was, "Go forth under the open sky, and list to nature's teachings."

List? I know poets are fond of shortening words to get them to fit the poem. Did he mean "listen"? Of course, we would be wise to listen to nature. But if we "list" as a boat might, we lean. In this instance we would lean towards nature; grow closer to it.

Bryant isn't around to ask about the meaning, but whether we listen to nature or list towards her, what matters is that we learn the lessons she has to offer. It's only natural, after all.

## Friday — August 25

DO you know what a rangoli is? It's a design drawn in ground corn outside Indian homes to symbolise welcome. They can be very colourful and amazingly intricate but, of course, little creatures eat them, the wind blows them and the feet of those being welcomed will wear them away.

We all have different ways of making people feel welcome, but if the rangoli teaches us anything it is this – our hospitality should constantly be refreshed and renewed and out front for everyone to see.

## Saturday — August 26

HELEN had discovered it was her favourite author's birthday, and indulged in some cake to celebrate!

If you look at the number of special days already being celebrated nationally and internationally, and then you add birthdays of family and friends, and then add in anniversaries that mean something to you personally, some favourite events in history, even birthdays of favourite authors . . . it should be possible to find something to celebrate every day of the year.

Imagine that! A year of celebration! But a word of advice, if I may. You don't always need to celebrate with cake!

## Sunday — August 27

THERE'S an old parenting dictum that goes "a child needs your love most when he or she deserves it least."

The same thinking could be applied to adults. Would anyone really choose to be like that if there wasn't a hurt or unhappiness deep inside them?

Perhaps Jesus had something similar in mind when he said, "You have heard that it was said, you shall love your neighbour and hate your enemy. But I say to you, love your enemies and pray for those who persecute you."

## Monday — August 28

IT is a real blessing to be able to say the comforting thing to someone struggling with difficult times. But those words don't always fly quickly to the tongue. It can be very tempting to walk away rather than run the risk of saying the wrong thing. But we mustn't.

For those of us who would still be of use when useful words are nowhere to be found, I offer this thought from the hymnwriter Frederick William Faber –

"As well as the grace of kind speaking there is also the grace of kind listening."

A bower of joy.

## Tuesday — August 29

**M**ARTIN is not romantic. He believes real romance lies in the little details – the kindnesses, the tolerance, the consideration.

Generally, his wife Cora agrees, yet she has always had a hankering for love letters tied up in ribbon. But the men of his family never went in for such nonsense. His grandad had written his grandmother one letter – with a stub of pencil on the back of a receipt he wrote how much he missed her.

Cora pointed out that his grandmother had kept that for over forty years. So Martin booked a hotel room for a night in a neighbouring town. Finding he really did miss Cora, he wrote it all down. And in the envelope he put a ribbon!

## Wednesday — August 30

**I** WOULD guess that when Isaac Pennington wrote these words he was talking about his fellow Quakers.

"Our life is love and peace, and tenderness, and bearing with one another, and forgiving one another, and not laying accusations one against another."

But perhaps he was talking about you and me. Do you wish that those words did apply to your life? I know I do.

Love, peace, tenderness, forgiveness; we can all do those things but can we make a life of them? Let's try.

## Thursday — August 31

**A** FRIEND and I walked along the banks of a river. A swan stood on the mud-flats. It was asleep with its head tucked under its wing. It had raised one leg, leaving it perfectly balanced on the other.

"There's a lesson there!" my friend said. "That swan is its own comfort and support, as we should be!"

But I much prefer the old Irish proverb, "It is in the shelter of each other that people live."

Then I challenged him to stand on one leg with his head under his arm. And, to give him credit, he tried!

# September

## Friday — September 1

THERE are many churches dedicated to Saint Giles, including one on the Royal Mile, near Edinburgh Castle. There is a tradition that churches dedicated to the saint, who was supposedly left lame by a hunting accident, should be on the edge of town, or on a main thoroughfare (such as the Royal Mile) so that people in need, struggling with infirmities, could reach them more easily.

Some organisations, and people, prefer to be off the beaten path, more difficult to reach – and perhaps that serves their purposes well. We should be a little obscure, a little hidden away, if that's what our mission calls for. But, on Saint Giles's Day and the rest of the year, let us reserve a special appreciation for the ones who set out to help and put themselves right in the midst of those who need it.

## Saturday — September 2

BEFORE hiring a new worker, the farmer asked what he could do. "I can sleep through a storm," the labourer said. It didn't make any sense to the farmer but he needed a worker and, for the next few months, the man was perfectly capable.

Then a storm struck in the middle of the night. The farmer jumped out of bed and ran into the rain. He banged on the door of the labourer's cottage but got no answer, so he ran off to try to minimise the damage the storm would cause.

But he found the animals were in the barn, the machinery and tools were stowed away, all the doors were locked, and the thatched roof the labourer had repaired was riding out the storm nicely.

Then he understood. The labourer could sleep through a storm, whenever it arrived, because he knew he had done his work properly.

Storms come in all walks of life. Do your best during the day and you will always sleep well at night.

## Sunday — September 3

A LICE ROOSEVELT LONGWORTH was the oldest daughter of President Theodore Roosevelt and she had a simple philosophy which she maintained throughout her long life. It was, "Fill what is empty, empty what is full – and scratch where it itches."

Humanity has always looked for a simple philosophy. I like, "Give more than you take. Fix more than you break."

But for something more substantial, and almost as short, my favourite just has to be these words from the Book of John as spoken by Jesus: "A new command I give you: love one another. As I have loved you, so you must love one another."

There's a "philosophy" that genuinely will take care of everything.

## Monday — September 4

THE village of Rjukan in Norway is a lovely place, but the mountains to the south of it block out direct sunlight for a large part of the year, making it physically a pretty gloomy place to live.

Thankfully, the inhabitants also have mountains to the north. Now an array of computer-controlled, solar-powered mirrors reflects the sun's light down into the village square.

Someone who lived there said, "We did sort of get used to the shade. But this is so warming. Not just physically, but mentally."

If you have a blessing in your life then be the mirror that shares it with someone in a darker place. Then watch them grow because of it.

## Tuesday — September 5

WHEN Stephen Hawking wrote his book on the nature of time he wanted it to be accessible to the average reader. But it's a safe bet that even his "simple" explanation went over the heads of most of the people who bought the book.

Now, I'm no scientist. But he did say one thing I could understand!

"Remember to look up at the stars and not down at your feet."

## Wednesday — September 6

*I LOVE the gorgeous autumn woods,*
*The glorious chestnut trees,*
*The gentle thump as conkers fall*
*And boys scoop up with glee.*
*I love the curling woodsmoke*
*And the harvest atmosphere,*
*The mellow tones, the muted shades,*
*This special time of year.*
*The trees are glowing red and gold,*
*They set the lanes aflame,*
*How wonderful, sweet autumn,*
*To see you here again.*

– Dorothy McGregor.

## Thursday — September 7

THESE days you can find gurus teaching all sorts of things. They will teach you how to get ahead in business, how to stop smoking or lose weight, how to "cosmically" attract your heart's desire, and so on. Of course, much of it is nonsense.

The poet and philosopher Lao Tzu lived in China around 600 BC. He reckoned he could teach people how to find treasure!

"I have just three things to teach," he wrote, "simplicity, patience, compassion. These three are your greatest treasures."

## Friday — September 8

THERE are troubles in every life and we console ourselves with the ancient wisdom, "This, too, shall pass." But my friend Alison, who hails from the Caribbean, tells me of a local version of the saying.

"Day will run till moon ketch 'um." The moon being the peace that eventually "ketched" and overtook all our worries.

The troubles of the day will have their say but, one way or another, peace generally catches up with them and washes them away.

And I dare say a good night's sleep under the Caribbean moon would help as well!

## Saturday — September 9

DO you ever look at paintings in galleries and think, I wish I could make something so beautiful? Well, masterpieces take years of specialised training and practice – not to mention a spark of creative genius – to create. Things well beyond us ordinary folk.

But wait! In one of his essays Ralph Waldo Emerson wrote, "A friend may well be reckoned the masterpiece of nature."

Have you ever been a friend? Well, there is a masterpiece right there! And you may well have created more masterpieces than any creative geniuses throughout history.

## Sunday — September 10

THIS world is full of marvellous abilities. Think of all the talents other people have. Wouldn't it be nice to be able to paint, build, juggle, write, design, dance like they do?

Voltaire suggested we take another approach.

"Appreciation is a wonderful thing," he wrote. "It makes what is excellent in others belong to us, too."

And, of course, we don't need to stop at talents and abilities. Everything that is excellent should be fair game for our appreciation.

As the Apostle John said, "Brothers and sisters, whatever is true, whatever is noble, whatever is right, whatever is pure, whatever is lovely, whatever is admirable – if anything is excellent or praiseworthy – think about such things."

## Monday — September 11

HOPE. What's the point of it? If you've done all you can do then surely you should just give up.

Charles Dickens put it like this: "Always hope; never leave off hoping; don't leave a stone unturned. It's always something to know you've done the most you could. But don't leave off hoping, or it's no use doing anything. Hope, hope to the last!"

It's almost a shame that these words come from "Nicholas Nickleby", because hope surely is the Great Expectation.

## Tuesday — September 12

ALEXANDER DUMAS JUNIOR was born illegitimate in a time when that was a great social stigma. His father, the celebrated author, had him educated at a private school where his family status brought him regular ridicule. Friends were few and far between, but they were more greatly valued because of this.

Dumas the Younger wrote, "Friendship consists in forgetting what one gives, and remembering what one receives."

His father also penned a definition of friendship when he gave his Musketeers their famous rallying call, "All for one, and one for all!"

## Wednesday — September 13

TALKING with older people (and yes, there are a few who are older than me), I notice a strange thing. Their fondest recollections are often associated with difficult times.

I have a theory, though, and it is supported by these words from Helen Keller, the deaf and blind woman who went on to become an author and an inspirational speaker.

"The world," she wrote, "is full of suffering. It is also full of the overcoming of it."

It's not, I believe, the hard times we remember so fondly. It is the overcoming of them, the times we achieved the impossible, the times we all pulled together. Those abiding memories are the gifts difficult times leave behind.

## Thursday — September 14

ROBERT LOUIS STEVENSON saw more of the world than many living at the same time, and his writer's mind paid close attention to each new wonder along the way.

"The best things," Stevenson wrote, "are the nearest. Breath in your nostrils, light in your eyes, flowers at your feet, duties at your hand, the path of God just before you."

I don't doubt he was right but, still, it would be nice to go to Hawaii and a few of the other places he went – just to make sure.

## Friday — September 15

CAN there be any "up-side" to bad times? Well, in the long term we are reassured that difficult times make us stronger, but perhaps without those times we wouldn't need to be stronger. So, those might cancel each other out.

No, I'm thinking about a more tangible benefit. The proof that there are people round about you who will reach out a supportive hand, who will walk and work with you, who will simply sit and listen when that's what you need.

Without the bad times . . . Well, Charles Dickens put it this way, "But for some trouble and sorrow we should never know half the good there is about us."

The price may be a difficult one to pay, but the results will often take a broken heart, heal it, fill it, and set you about your way more hopeful than before because you know there is love in the world.

## Saturday — September 16

HOW can you tell if someone is wise just by looking at them? Might those wrinkles on their forehead imply a lot of thought? They might. Or they might not.

For certainty, I tend towards the old German proverb that suggests, "Continual cheerfulness is the sign of wisdom." Isn't it a comfort to know that the wisest tend towards the notion that everything is working out as it should – and it is good?

## Sunday — September 17

SOMETIMES children take Bible lessons literally. And sometimes we can learn from them as they struggle to learn for themselves.

A puzzled girl asked her mother if it was true that, as she had heard, God was bigger than any of us. He mother assured her that He was. But the Sunday School teacher had also told the girl that God lives in each of us.

"If that's true," she asked her mum, "wouldn't He show through?"

It's up to each of us to make sure that, in our case, He does!

**Time to reflect.**

## Monday — September 18

DO you remember when we used to hem things or have them hemmed for us?

Then came an ingenious way of hemming things with an iron and a special strip instead of a needle and thread.

And now clothes, like so many things, seem to be worn for a while and replaced long before they wear out. So, does anyone still hem? I think we all should.

A wise man (or more likely a wise woman) once said, "Hem your blessings with thankfulness, so they don't unravel."

## Tuesday — September 19

THERE'S an old tale about a busybody who noticed she had new, young neighbours. She didn't introduce herself, she just watched them through her window.

When the woman hung a whites wash out she couldn't believe how grey they looked. She decided she needed to give the young folk the benefit of her wisdom.

But when she stepped out of her door she noticed the sheets were suddenly bright and white. The problem, it turned out, was that her own windows were rather grimy, giving the world a grey tinge.

I wonder if the playwright George Bernard Shaw knew the lady in question. He wrote, "Better keep yourself clean and bright. You are the window through which you see the world."

## Wednesday — September 20

JUST because a comedian says something for a laugh doesn't mean it has to be taken at all seriously. So, when the man on the stage said, "Relationships give you a reason to live. And that reason is revenge!" I groaned as I dutifully cracked a smile.

I have no idea if his next joke was better because I was too busy rewriting that one in my head based on my personal experience.

Relationships do give you a reason to live. And I've always found that reason to be gratitude.

## Thursday — September 21

ON this day in 1915 Cecil Chubb, the son of a village saddle-maker, happened upon an auction where a ring of impressive stones was being sold. Chubb thought his wife might like it so he paid £6,600 for Lot 51.

Unhappily, so the story goes, his wife didn't like the ring. So he gave it to the government on condition it be preserved as it was. And so Stonehenge came into public ownership!

In making its preservation a condition of the gift he tried to make sure that the stone ring, like diamonds, would be for ever.

His wife might have appreciated a diamond ring more, but the nation will always have cause to appreciate Cecil Chubb's generosity – and his slightly misguided idea of a romantic gift.

## Friday — September 22

SOMETIMES we do a thing without thinking to name it. But a name is always a useful thing, helping us to share or organise whatever it is. So, might I offer you a name for something I am sure you have done to one degree or another at this time of year?

Momijigari. "Gari" is Japanese for "hunting" and "momiji" means "red leaves". It's a tradition there to go as a family to the places with the prettiest autumnal displays just to enjoy the colours.

Now . . . if only there was a word to be had for the fun that comes from kicking through a pile of those leaves!

## Saturday — September 23

TOWN mottoes might be a bit passé these days but they are an indicator that people once had aspirations worth adopting; worth carving in stone on some significant monument or building.

Some of them still have the power to make us stop and think. On a recent visit to the beautiful town of Millport on the Isle of Cumbrae I noticed that their town motto was "Altiora Videnda", which translates as "Aspiring to all things noble or high".

May they – and we – keep reaching for the heights.

## Sunday — September 24

THEY say that the word "lady" comes, through some convoluted pronunciation, from the ancient term "hlaf-dig", which means "bread-dispenser". I suppose the idea back then was that the man, the farmer, would be the "bread-winner" and his wife would bake it and distribute it. The ladies of note would be the ones who had enough to distribute beyond the bounds of their own family to the poor and needy. Thus, the term "lady" acquired a little more dignity than the humbler "woman" or "wife".

At this time of Harvest Thanksgiving let us appreciate what we have, and go further if we can, sharing with those who might be struggling, whether we give food or other assistance, whether we be a gentleman or a hlaf-dig.

## Monday — September 25

VISITING a friend's house, I noticed she had a beautifully decorated strip of cloth hanging on her wall. I hadn't seen it before so I asked what the Japanese writing on it meant.

She translated it as, "Each step is the place to learn."

I took a step closer to the wall-hanging and startled a butterfly I had assumed was part of the design. As it fluttered around us I understood I had learned something in that step at least. Even if it was only to wear my glasses more often!

Whether we walk, ride or shuffle, may we always be learning – and admiring – as we go.

## Tuesday — September 26

IN the 19th century it was the done thing for people of means to go on a "grand tour" of Europe. The writer Emily Kinbrough and her friend Cornelia did their tour in the 1920s.

"Remember," Ms Kinbrough wrote, "we all stumble. That's why it's a comfort to go hand in hand."

Often I take the Lady of the House's hand over some rough ground – and she catches me when I stumble. I'm sure it's a comfort for both of us.

Peaceful pathway.

## Wednesday — September 27

**I AM** always on the lookout for new definitions of friendships. This one was found, handwritten around a photograph of two deck-chairs sitting side by side, in a holiday cottage by the coast.

I couldn't help but feel the anonymous poet/artist knew what he or she was talking about. They must have had a few such moments in mind – and I hope you do, too.

*When the coffee is hot*, the inscription went, *and the talk is good, and the feeling is easy, and the laughter is light, and the memories are many, but the time is too short . . . then you know you are with a friend.*

And I couldn't help but imagine that many a good coffee goes happily cold in times like that.

## Thursday — September 28

**I'VE** heard of groups like this before and I hope to hear of more, but the Nine Nanas are such a fine example of it.

Thirty-five years ago the ladies, who call themselves sisters despite not being related, decided they wanted to be like their own grandparents, who always seemed to be helping folk.

Working on the principle that everyone ought to have a grandparent to help them, they started doing extra baking, saving a little money here and there, making the most of the sales, and anything else that occurred to them.

Then, whenever they heard of a mum who was struggling, or a widow who couldn't make ends meet, or a family with too many bills to pay, they would help, but always anonymously.

Until, after thirty years of keeping it a secret, one of their husbands found out. And since they went public they have helped even more people.

People are wonderfully inventive in the ways they find to help each other. I imagine there is a group carrying on the tradition of helping neighbours somewhere near you.

Or you and your friends might even be about to start one!

## Friday — September 29

DASHIELL HAMMETT wrote many detective novels in the 1920s and 1930s. It was one of his characters, the private investigator Sam Spade, I believe, who said, "You got to look on the bright side – even if there isn't one."

We can say there is no redeeming feature to a situation and settle for that, but the thing about people who relentlessly look for the positive in life is if they can't find it, they usually make it.

And the world is better because of their refusal to settle for less.

Sam Spade had probably had enough of dark alleys and dastardly deeds to appreciate a little "bright side".

And haven't we all. The question is, can we shine bright enough to banish even some little shadows? And if we can, don't you think we ought to?

## Saturday — September 30

*DOWN the hillside we ambled, observing,*
*In the haze of the afternoon sun,*
*One could scarcely tell where the sky ended,*
*And hills, land and sea were as one.*

*But, parting the mists with its wonder,*
*There rippled a pool of pure gold,*
*And a small boat was lazily drifting*
*As we watched the vision unfold.*

*We cherished that beautiful moment.*
*In this world, the hours must move on,*
*And soon now the sun would be setting.*
*For ever this time would be gone.*

*But we'd had a glimpse of Life fairer*
*To carry when this day was done.*
*Ours always to keep and remember*
*In the glow of the September sun.*

– Marion Cleworth.

# October

## Sunday — October 1

THE church of Santa Johann in Val di Funes looks like an artist's depiction of a humble little mountain-country church. It looks like it might seat twenty people at the most and is raised slightly higher than the wild-flower meadow around it.

But visitors to the church, on a clear day, usually spend more time outside it than in it. You see, this little piece of man-made artistry and devotion sits amidst the breathtakingly beautiful Dolomite Mountains on a grassy plateau, fringed by forest and overlooked by steeply rising mountains which are a World Natural Heritage Site.

The places man makes to worship God can be wonderful, but none is anywhere near as inspiring as the Lord's own work.

## Monday — October 2

*MY friend said, "Remember the old days,*
*When we were both supple and lean?*
*"We followed those video workouts,*
*We had a good fitness routine!"*
*"We can't play those now," I said sadly.*
*Then, much to our mutual glee,*
*We searched on the net and discovered*
*Those workouts were on DVD!*
*It's certainly jogged some old memories*
*As our new twice-weekly drill proves:*
*As soon as we started, we realised*
*That we could recall all the moves!*
*Now we're getting fitter together*
*It's so great to share this again:*
*We're marching and jumping and skipping*
*Our way down old memory lane!*

– Emma Canning.

## Tuesday — October 3

AMOS BRONSON ALCOTT was a 19th-century educator who pioneered new, less authoritarian teaching methods. Instead of dictating he preferred to interact with his students.

It's a style that is much more common now, so it is difficult to imagine how revolutionary it must have seemed back then. I am sure his was a popular class and many of his students probably considered him a friend.

He said, "Stay is a charming word in a friend's vocabulary."

A small word, of no apparent consequence, but it conveys a spirit of welcome, acceptance and the promise of good conversation.

Just not, perhaps, if you are being told to "stay" after class.

## Wednesday — October 4

THERE is an old Greek maxim, which translates as, "Love your friend with his fault."

Wait . . . what? That assumes your friend has a fault, and a specific one at that. Well, doesn't he (or she)? Everyone does and if we ended friendships over the fact then we would have none.

So, as the saying advises, love your friend with his fault. You can be sure your friend is doing the same for you.

## Thursday — October 5

HARRY was waiting patiently while his wife talked to friends.

"I feel like the Mona Lisa's frame," he told me when I wandered over. "No-one pays the least attention to me, but I get to hold and support one of the world's most beautiful women."

Actually, that frame is pretty special, too. It's a gift, made a century ago, from the Comtesse de Béhague.

Of course people viewing the two together will tend to focus on the picture, but the painting and frame add value to each other; they depend on each other. Just like Harry and his wife. Just like any good marriage.

## Friday — October 6

IN general we are born, grow up and go out into the world hoping to achieve many different things; some good, some bad, some self-serving, some noble and some for the greater good.

I have a feeling there would be less of the negative and more of the positive if every nursery or childhood bedroom were inscribed with these words by Hilaire Belloc.

"From quiet homes and first beginnings
Out to the undiscovered ends,
There's nothing worth the wear of winning
But laughter and the love of friends."

## Saturday — October 7

WHEN he was 81 and she was 75 the Canadian poet and social activist F.R. Scott and his wife Marian could still be seen "holding hands and swinging them like happy children." Their long marriage was described as "something creative in the art of living."

You and I might not be artists but the example Mr and Mrs Scott set reminds us that these lives are ours to sculpt, paint or write as we will. Our hugs might be seen as couplets, our smiles as bold brush strokes, with hands held together as our finest carvings.

It's a fanciful notion, to be sure, but why wouldn't we want to be creative with our love and paint a beautiful image of our lives?

## Sunday — October 8

HENRY VAN DYKE wrote, "Time is too slow for those who wait, too swift for those who fear, too long for those who grieve, too short for those who rejoice. But for those who love, time is not."

How can that be?

Well, time hasn't always been around. Scientists and theologians agree there was a time before time, when the faithful would have it there was only God. And what are we told He is? God is love.

Those of us who love or are loved or have anything to do with love are taking part in something that outlasts even time itself.

## Monday — October 9

WE were talking about the latest trip by a mutual friend who seems to have been most places in the world. That's when my dear friend Mary got that familiar twinkle in her eye.

"You know, Francis," she said. "On most of the really important journeys in my life I've never gone the whole distance.

"I'm not talking about physically travelling anywhere. But the most worthwhile journeys I have ever made have been to meet someone halfway."

The scenery might not be much to look at, and the timing is almost never convenient, but it's always a trip worth making.

## Tuesday — October 10

AS President of the United States when the world was at war, Woodrow Wilson must have been more aware than most of the forces that separate us. Those were very troubled times with nations battling nations and political factions arguing. But he also knew what would bring us together. It wasn't trade, it wasn't power, or politics, or even talking.

The "cement that would hold the world together" was, he believed, friendship.

## Wednesday — October 11

EMPEROR TITUS of Rome was both an effective war leader and a benevolent ruler. Contemporary historians tended to favour him, but not every emperor wanted a reputation for kindness so perhaps they were simply being honest.

We might each take on board these words attributed to him by the historian Suetonius.

"Recalling after dinner that he had done nothing to help anyone all that day, he gave voice to that memorable remark: 'Friends, I have lost a day!'"

Instead of regretting a lost opportunity, surely it would be a better idea to look ahead to whom we could help next?

## Thursday — October 12

E.B. WHITE'S "Charlotte's Web" is a children's book enjoyed by as many adults. There's a line that always makes me pause to think. Wilbur asks Charlotte, "Why did you do all this for me? I've never done anything for you."

Charlotte replies, "You have been my friend. That, in itself, is a tremendous thing."

Don't forget to let your friends know that they are tremendous. And then pat yourself on the back for being tremendous, too.

## Friday — October 13

SISTER CORITA KENT had this advice on how to make the world a better place – "Love the moment and the energy of that moment will spread beyond all boundaries."

Love the people who are around you, whatever the situation. It will warm their day and they won't be able to help but pass it on.

So, when loving the world seems too much to ask, love the moment. Does it sound "hippy-dippy"? It possibly is, but it's my opinion that those hippies, and Sister Corita, might have known a thing or two about the power of love.

## Saturday — October 14

AS I stitch my patchwork quilt each piece makes me feel glad,
For every fabric represents a happy time I've had.
This blue piece was a tablecloth I made for dolly's tea,
I used to lay out fairy cakes and plastic cutlery.
The pink came from a costume that I wore in my school show,
Though how I got the leading role I really do not know!
The yellow was the dancing dress I wore when I met Bill.
He said that I looked beautiful. He's just as loving still.
Stitching them together, I feel so content, just knowing
That all my special memories live in the quilt I'm sewing.

– Susannah White.

Your dreams are just over the horizon.

## Sunday — October 15

THE Tree Church in New Zealand is exactly what it sounds like.

Its "builder" loved trees and was also a fan of church architecture. So, it seemed like the obvious thing to do to plant some trees and grow them into the shape of a church. Now it's a visitor attraction and a popular wedding venue.

A gimmick? It would be easy to say so. But people who have been there talk about the sense of peace they come away with. It's a building that's a living part of Creation. Where better than that to worship the Creator?

## Monday — October 16

RALPH WALDO EMERSON is too great a thinker for me to take issue with – usually! He wrote – "The purpose of life is not to be happy. It is to be useful, to be honourable, to be compassionate, to have it make some difference that you have lived and lived well."

But perhaps that is what Mr Emerson was getting at after all; that happiness, rather than being a goal in its own right, is a wonderful by-product of a life lived to good purpose.

## Tuesday — October 17

AMY runs a tea-shop. After reading a lot about oriental tea ceremonies she decided a lot of it wouldn't work in her shop for practical reasons, but she did retain the notion of "ichi-go ichi-e."

It translates as "for this time only" or "one chance in a lifetime." With that in mind she gives her best in each and every transaction.

Imagine if, every time we met or talked to someone, each time we bent our attention to some task, we understood that this moment would never be again, that it was a once in a lifetime opportunity to make a good impression or do a good job.

How would that change your life? For the better, I am sure. How much of a difference it made would depend on how much you are already making of this moment. Something worth thinking about over a cup of tea, I'd say.

## Wednesday — October 18

AS well as being an Oscar-winning actress and a world-famous celebrity, Sophia Loren is also a mother of two.

She said, "When you are a mother, you are never really alone in your thoughts. A mother always has to think twice, once for herself and once for her child."

We often aren't at our best when we think only of ourselves. We take chances, we cut corners, we can be careless. But give us someone else to worry about, and we really rise to the occasion.

Those second thoughts are more important than they might seem – at first thought!

## Thursday — October 19

HAVE you ever felt *gezellig*?

Don't worry, it's not something you might visit the doctor for. Dutch friends tell me it's their name for the feeling you get when you are surrounded by loved ones, everyone is happy and healthy, and the world seems to be a fine place to live in.

Now that I have described it I am sure you are nodding and know exactly what *gezellig* is.

And do you know what else is a *gezellig* feeling? The fact that cultures around the world might be different, languages are different, some have words that other don't have, but the whole world has the same emotions and feelings in common.

## Friday — October 20

HAVE you ever made a new friend and noticed that the world seems so much brighter because of it? Perhaps that's down to how wonderful the friend is, but the new "light" might equally well have come from you. It may have been there all along, waiting for the right friend to turn it on.

The Spanish philosopher Miguel de Unamuno put it this way – "A new friend enriches our spirit not so much by what he gives of himself as by what he causes us to discover in our own selves."

## Saturday — October 21

THE secret of happiness? Many people claim to have discovered it. But it depends on what kind of happiness you mean. There is the momentary burst of delight or the slow-burning candle of contentment. Do you want happiness for a day or for a lifetime?

I liked Helen Keller's take on the latter. Having become deaf and blind, happiness might have been in short supply in her life. But she went on to become a writer, an inspirational public speaker and the champion of many social causes.

She believed that many people had the wrong idea of what constituted "true happiness".

"It is not to be attained through self-gratification," she wrote, "but through fidelity to a worthy purpose."

In other words, find something worth doing and stick to it!

## Sunday — October 22

WILLIAM CAREY was a missionary in India in the late 18th century. When he first proposed the idea he was told, "If God wants to save anyone in India he will do it without your help or ours!"

It reminded me of a church in France which was bombed during World War II and the hands and feet of a statue of Christ were damaged. The parishioners decided not to repair the statue as they themselves would be the hands and feet of the Lord.

God does have work to do and He chooses to do it through us, whether on missions abroad or on missions to our neighbour's house.

## Monday — October 23

EMELIE DU CHÂTELET was an 18th-century mathematician and physicist. As a mathematician you might expect her to plot an exact route to where she wanted to go. But she was more concerned with the journey than the destination and suggested we "sow that route with flowers."

Wherever your journeys take you, travel in such a way that there will be flowers of welcome to enjoy should you ever return there.

## Tuesday — October 24

MYRTIE BARKER lived alone after her parents died, declaring her intention to be "a good hermitess." That hermit status was soon compromised by her good heart when she invited one destitute widow to live with her. And then another.

Explaining the difference between her original intention and how things actually worked out, she said, "The idea of strictly minding your own business is mouldy rubbish. Who could be so heartless?"

As Myrtie showed, minding our own business doesn't necessarily mean cutting ourselves off from others. Instead the good hermitess chose to make people her business – and then she minded them!

## Wednesday — October 25

THE term "clock-watching" has become synonymous with getting nothing done. But we might actually get a good deal done if we watched the clock with a view to doing what it does.

Have a look and you'll notice – it never goes backwards, doesn't dwell in the past, it is consistent and it accomplishes big works in little steps by always moving forward.

Let us, likewise, be ever onwards! One tick, or tock, at a time!

## Thursday — October 26

WILLIAM TEMPLE was a social reformer, who, when no-one was lending any credence to the plight of Jews in Germany during the war, berated Parliament about it.

When he was at school his father wrote to him, saying, "I would strongly urge you, my dear lad, always to stand on your own ground. You know right and wrong better than many boys, for few mothers have taken the pains your mother has done with you. Don't be moved, shoved, pushed, laughed off your own ground by any number of boys."

Can parents do more for their children than show them a good place to stand and provide them with the encouragement to keep it and to build on it?

## Friday — October 27

WOULD you believe there is a museum in Zagreb devoted to broken relationships? The museum contains donated artifacts from love affairs gone wrong: break-up letters, notes written in desperation, unworn wedding dresses . . .

The idea came about when two artists, ending a four-year affair, joked that they would need a museum to house everything that reminded them of each other.

Strangely, it turns out to be quite an inspirational place. Love, like so many good things, it seems, is often taken for granted. Seeing how easily it can go wrong reminds us of how precious it really is!

## Saturday — October 28

THE world owes a debt of gratitude to Jonas Salk, who was born on this day in 1914. He was the inventor of the polio vaccine. Salk could have become a millionaire overnight by patenting the vaccine – but he didn't.

When asked about that decision he replied, "Could you patent the sun?" Like sunshine, he wanted his vaccine to be free (or as cheap as possible) for all humanity.

Salk's legacy was a vaccine that saved millions of lives. He also reminds us that the abiding legacy of good times and dreams is that we can still draw strength from them decades after.

## Sunday — October 29

LOOK up at the stained-glass windows in Liverpool's Anglican cathedral and you might see Josephine Butler, who was a great champion of women and their causes in the 19th century.

Her passion for improving the lot of women by increasing their chances of fair and equitable treatment may have stemmed from the death, at a young age, of her own daughter.

Which thought casts a new light on these words of hers – "Take of the very stones over which you have stumbled and fallen, and use them to pave your road to Heaven."

## Monday — October 30

HAVE you heard of "the Laughing Philosopher"?
Democritus lived in Rome about 350 years BC. He may have been the one of the first people to come up with the idea that the world was created from atoms.

And how did that affect his demeanour? Well, legend has it he laughed so often and so much that the people thought he must have gone crazy. They called another great philosopher, Hippocrates, to have a word with him.

The two men spent a while discussing life and human nature, then Hippocrates left – laughing!

So, what did they see that caused them such hilarity? Far be it from me to venture a guess, but I can add one small observation of my own. You see, there are two main reasons for laughing at something – either you find it ridiculous, or you find it wonderful!

There are many out there who choose the former option, thinking life is ridiculous. To them I say, follow the example of the Laughing Philosopher, the discoverer of atomic theory . . . and look closer!

## Tuesday — October 31

THE artist Michelangelo famously said, "Every block of stone has a statue inside it and it is the task of the sculptor to discover it."

But there still are, in Italian museums, uncompleted works of Michelangelo where only a hand or a leg or a head are visible. For whatever reason, the great master never completely found the statue in those blocks.

It's hard to look at those blocks of stone without wondering what might have come from them had Michelangelo kept chiselling.

It's even more difficult to contemplate a life that, for whatever reason, hasn't fulfilled its full potential.

Perhaps time or work or family responsibilities or fear has kept someone from being all they can be. But underneath all of those things lies a work of art. Sometimes we just have to be our own sculptor. And keep chiselling!

# November

MANY of us think that society has become far too disposable. Things are often replaced by newer models these days before they are used up or worn out.

Harry reckons civilisation has always struggled to find a balance between the old and the new.

"Some things," he pontificated, "are very old but still work well and the world would have a difficult time replacing them."

I have my "wise" moments as well and I raised a hand to let him know I knew he was talking about himself.

"The sun and the moon, for instance," he finished.

And I shoved my hand back into my pocket.

CHARLES DICKENS lived in England in the 19th century. Brother Lawrence lived in France in the 17th century. The first was a celebrity in his time, the second was a monk living a life of poverty. But I think they would have liked each other.

Brother Lawrence was known for doing the humblest task – be it scrubbing pots or repairing sandals – happily as an offering to God. His chores were, in a way, his daily offerings and prayers.

Dickens must have shared a similar view and would certainly have understood Brother Lawrence's philosophy.

"There is surely something charming," he wrote, "in the sight of the smallest thing done so thoroughly as if to remind the careless that whatever is worth doing is worth doing well."

The last eight words have since become part of the everyday vocabulary.

If only the spirit of the whole quote by Dickens and the way of life exemplified by Brother Lawrence were as well known.

Finding the balance.

## Friday — November 3

THE wisdom of Mohandas (Mahatma) Gandhi was respected around the world. But he himself didn't think too highly of it!

"It is unwise to be too sure of one's own wisdom," he said. "It is healthy to be reminded that the strongest might weaken and the wisest might err."

We might know what a man or woman is today, but we often don't know what they were yesterday, or how far they might go tomorrow!

## Saturday — November 4

IMAGINE the sheer audacity of Orville and Wilbur Wright! They were going to prove a heavy machine could fly through the air – despite the fact that all the preceding generations had almost unanimously decided such a thing was impossible. What courage and determination it must have taken to defy those odds!

Talking about their success, Orville Wright said, "If we all worked on the assumption that what was accepted as true were really true there would be no hope of advance."

The Wright brothers redefined the general perception of truth in one area. Surely we can do the same in another. Trust, love, hope, fly!

## Sunday — November 5

DO you worry about the future? People have always done it. Even in Ancient Greece, 500 years before Christ, concern about what was to come caused the playwright Aeschylus to comment on it.

"The future you shall know when it comes," he wrote. "Until then – forget about it!"

Or, as Jesus said in the Sermon on the Mount, "Therefore do not worry about tomorrow, for tomorrow will worry about itself. Each day has enough trouble of its own."

God has it under control. He always has and He always will.

## Monday — November 6

SOMEONE once said, "Where we love is home." I found myself wondering just what they meant by that. Did he or she mean that where we loved someone became a home of sorts, or was he talking about a particular place where we loved to be?

It occurred to me that there was an element of home in both of those feelings – and in just about every other way we might love. So perhaps, in the end, it is Love that is our real home.

I can't think of a better place to spend my days. Can you?

## Tuesday — November 7

A WISE man once said, "Courtesies of a small and trivial character are the ones which strike deepest in the grateful and appreciative heart."

I find it is just those little courtesies that best get through the defences of a hardened and unappreciative heart.

A little, unexpected kindness is sometimes all it takes to remind someone that they are, even after all they have done, still a part of the family. And having felt a little of it, they often lay down their shields voluntarily to feel some more of it.

Little courtesies. Sometimes there is nothing little about them!

## Wednesday — November 8

WISDOM suggests that when you don't know what to do, it's better to do something than to do nothing. But there are times when doing nothing isn't actually doing nothing.

Georges-Louis Leclerc was seen as "the father of all thought in natural history." If his studies taught him anything it was that the world and its Creator played the long game.

"Never think that God's delays are God's denials. Hold on; hold fast; hold out. Patience is genius."

So, it's wise to do nothing – if what you are actually doing is waiting for that answer.

## Thursday — November 9

IN Scots, the word "gang" has nothing to do with a group of people. It means "to go," and is sometimes translated as "walk." Which helps us understand the beautiful old saying, "Kindness creeps where it canna gang."

In other words, kindness will always get to where it is most needed. And if the quickest, most direct way is blocked, it will simply find another way.

The way we want to help someone isn't always the way they need to be helped. So, if you can't "gang" don't hesitate to "creep."

## Friday — November 10

THERE'S a story of a Lord Mayor of long ago who had his portrait painted. When the work was finished he looked at it, and in a fit of anger declared it looked nothing like him. He refused to pay, told the artist he would never do another portrait in that city, and asked what he was going to do about it.

The bemused artist agreed that perhaps he had been guilty of idealising the Lord Mayor's looks.

"It probably doesn't do you justice, sir," he said. "But perhaps if you spent a year or two calming your temper, thinking finer thoughts, and being kinder to your fellow man . . . you might come to look like it."

## Saturday — November 11

THE author C.S. Lewis served as a soldier during World War I. In a radio broadcast during World War II he suggested that soldiering encompassed all the woes and fears of life.

"Like sickness," he said, "it threatens pain and death. Like poverty, it threatens ill lodging, cold, heat, thirst and hunger. Like slavery, it threatens toil, humiliation, injustice and arbitrary rule. Like exile, it separates you from all you love."

On Remembrance Day, let us remember to love, so we need mourn no more.

## Sunday — November 12

REMEMBRANCE DAY, just past, is also Saint Martin's Day. Martin was a soldier who saw Christ after he gave his military cloak to a freezing beggar. He went on to become Bishop of Tours.

We love God when we show kindness to a brother or sister regardless of their station and whether they deserve it or not. The kindness is the thing.

Martin saw Jesus when he put that teaching into action. For those who do the same but don't see the Lord appear in person, maybe they should look into their own hearts. He is bound to be there.

## Monday — November 13

HE doesn't have enough sense to come in when it rains."

I have been caught out in some beautiful rain showers. Walking in the rain when we are prepared can be a very satisfying experience. Sometimes the rain can wash the soul clean as it washes the world.

Sense shouldn't necessarily be about coming in when it rains. It might be more about understanding that the beauty and wonder of nature isn't always dry.

## Tuesday — November 14

HAVE you ever heard of the Clever Dog Laboratory?

The trainers, in the Vienna Veterinary School, played a game with two dogs and gave them both a treat at the end. Then they changed the rules. Only one dog got the treat. The other dog refused to play any more.

It might seem like the dog was sulking but the people studying his reaction thought it went deeper than that. This was proof, they said, that dogs recognise unfairness and injustice. If that's the case then fairness must be something more than just a human concept.

A dog can only bark (or sulk) about such situations but we can speak up about them and in doing so end them.

Wouldn't that be a fine reward at the end of the "game"?

## Wednesday — November 15

*IT'S been a quiet sort of day: I read my book, I watched TV,*
*I listened to the radio; I saw a friend who came for tea.*
*We took a general knowledge quiz. (I lost, alas, she's quite a sage.)*
*I picked up an old reference book, and idly read a random page.*
*I briefly searched the internet to solve some tricky crossword clues,*
*Then, with the paper, I relaxed to catch up with the daily news.*
*A quiet day, but happy, too, for all my time was so productive;*
*Filled with only little things, and yet, each one was so instructive!*
*Reading, watching, listening – each pastime, in its special way,*
*Brought knowledge, spellbinding and fresh – what new things*
*   have you learned today?*

*– Emma Canning.*

## Thursday — November 16

WHO doesn't enjoy a little nostalgia? The French novelist Sidonie-Gabrielle Colette certainly did. She wrote, "But the past, the beautiful past striped with sunshine, grey with mist, childish, blooming with hidden joy, bruised with sweet sorrow. Ah! If only I could resurrect one hour of that time, one alone – but which one?"

Which one would you choose? But that difficult decision doesn't have to be made while we can recall them all in memory and spend our lives in the present – making new memories!

## Friday — November 17

I REMEMBER reading about a slightly built soldier who was asked how far he could march carrying a full pack. His reply was, "Eight miles, sir. Twelve if there's a band!"

The Scottish philosopher and writer Thomas Carlyle would certainly have agreed and approved. He wrote, "Give us the man who sings at his work. He will do more in the same time – he will do it better – he will persevere longer. One is scarcely sensible of fatigue whilst he marches to a band!"

Joy is a fuel that not only helps us go further in life, but makes the trip that much more worthwhile.

## Saturday — November 18

THE poet Alexander Pope must have been in a thoughtful mood when he wrote about losing a friend. "In every friend (who goes) we lose a part of ourselves – the best part."

The poet W.B. Yeats, who lived almost two hundred years later, must have understood what Pope was getting at. He wrote, "Think where man's glory most begins and ends, and say my glory was I had such friends."

To paraphrase C.S. Lewis, friends aren't essential to life – but they are what make life worth living.

## Sunday — November 19

THERE'S an old Chinese proverb that talks about pulling on plants to help them grow. A farmer was so impatient for his crop that every day he tugged the plants just a little to help them grow. And it seemed to work. Until they fell over and died. Pulling them had certainly made them seem taller, but only at the expense of the roots which were continually being pulled out of the nourishing soil.

How many of us can sympathise with that farmer, even while acknowledging it was a foolish thing to do? Patience is sometimes one of the most difficult virtues, but that which God plants, in the fields or in our lives, will grow in God's time.

## Monday — November 20

RECENTLY saw pictures of ordinary beach sand magnified many times. I could see what looked like diamonds, rubies, emeralds – boring old sand never looked so fascinating.

I doubt if such powerful microscopes were available when William Blake wrote about the ability "to see the world in a grain of sand." But he was definitely on to something.

Sand is formed from worn-down rock. Rock is one of the basic building materials of the planet. It's quite a thought to know that, at a smaller level than we can see unaided, the world is made of such beauty!

## Tuesday — November 21

THE actor Woody Allen once said, "I'm astounded by people who want to know the universe when it's hard enough to find your way around Chinatown."

It might just have been a funny, throw-away line, but how well do you know the place you live in and the people you share it with?

On World Hello Day, when we are encouraged to say hello to at least ten people, why not take the chance to acquaint yourself with a few more of the people around you?

## Wednesday — November 22

THE Canadian astronaut Chris Hadfield described his flight into space on the space shuttle Endeavour. He recalled a lot of noise, vibration and fear. As the rocket flew faster, gravity tried to compress his rib-cage, leaving him thinking he might pass out.

But instead he reached that point of "zero-G" where all the weight fell away. Instead of fainting, he burst out laughing.

Many of us will know times when fears and pressures seem to be unbearable. Hold on! By the grace of God, with the help of friends, there will come a time when the pressure falls away – and then you'll be laughing!

## Thursday — November 23

YOU don't get something for nothing! I'm sure it's a universal law and a foundation of physics. And, therefore, these words of John of the Cross make no sense – "Where there is no love, pour love in and then you will draw love out."

Surely the love in equals the love out and so we are no better off. Until we consider the source of love and the fact that, if we have the heart, we can pour it and pour it without worrying about it running out.

And the love we give will always reward us in one way or another. So let us fill that well for others – and drink heartily from it ourselves knowing there will always be enough for everyone!

"Hello, there!"

## Friday — November 24

A PRANK was supposedly played by the great author H.G. Wells. He sent the same letter to dozens of the top men in society saying something like, "The game is up. They know everything."

It seems quite a few of them fled the country. What they were guilty of only they knew, but they were guilty of something.

Of course, we could spare ourselves that nagging guilt, that waiting to be discovered (even if it is only that we take too many biscuits from the barrel) by living a different sort of life; one where if "they know everything" you can say, "So, what?"

## Saturday — November 25

*DEAR Lord, I've been so busy, I've not had time to say*
*A thank you for the happiness that I've enjoyed today!*
*We all like looking forward to life's most pleasant things,*
*And fill each special moment with the memories it brings.*
*Yet when beset with problems we find some time for prayer,*
*Because we know God listens and shows his constant care.*
*Could we not then remember to spare the time to say*
*A thank you for the pleasure that we've received today?*

*– Elizabeth Gozney.*

## Sunday — November 26

THE old wisdom suggests you can light a thousand candles from one candle and the life of that candle will not be shortened.

I'm told it's a traditional Hawaiian prayer. I thought I would share it with you on this winter's day for the Hawaiian sunshine implicit in the first few images and the smile that's bound to come with the last one.

"May happiness, like trade winds, sustain you; may laughter, joyous as breakers, shake you; may strength, like coco-palms storm-bent, support you; and may the ancient shark of discontent disdain you." Amen!

## Monday — November 27

A MAN (I won't embarrass him by mentioning his name) was teaching his children how to have a relationship with God. He positioned the three of them at the foot of the basement stairs and he stood at the top.

"If you can get up here without touching the stairs," he said, "I will give you each ten pounds." The little exercise cost him thirty pounds.

"How did they do it?" I asked.

"They jumped on to a workbench," he explained, "climbed out a window and came in the back door of the house." I tried not to laugh as I asked how he had hoped they would do it. "They were supposed to ask me to carry them," he said. "Just like we should learn to fully depend on God."

"An excellent point," I conceded. Then my straight face slipped into a laugh as I added what the children already knew. "But God also provided the window and children smart enough to think of using it."

## Tuesday — November 28

WHAT comes to mind when I say the name Scrooge? I'm guessing the name conjured up some nasty images, but I'd like to suggest there was more to the man. Loss, fear and insecurity led him into a miserly lifestyle. As the ghost of Christmas future showed him, that downward spiral could only ever have one end.

But when forced to look at what his fears were doing to him he fought back. He made the change. He did better! And, thankfully, at least one of his family had waited for him.

The influences that kept Scrooge down work in many ways in many lives. The enduring popularity of the story shows that we want change for the better and believe it is possible.

Help is always available and we should be glad that it comes in friendlier forms than a spectral visitation. So, if you need to, make the change. You, too, can be the hero; the overcomer. Then you can look at the things that once held you back and say, "Bah, humbug!"

A WELL-KNOWN and oft-repeated quote from Samuel Johnson is, "A man, sir, should keep his friendship in constant repair."

It's usually taken as meaning we should look after the friends we have. And that's no bad thing. But the line before it cast a different light on Johnson's intentions.

He also said, "If a man does not make new acquaintance as he advances through life he will soon find himself left alone."

In other words, our friendship also might be a general thing and not limited to one friend or one set of friends.

But we should always be open to meeting new people in the hope that they might also become friends.

To use another familiar phrase that implies the same thing, "A stranger is just a friend you haven't made yet."

EVERY ten years the village of Oberammergau in Germany produces a Passion play, telling the story of the last days of Jesus Christ.

It's a powerful and world-famous production which is repeated every day over a five-month period, but I was particularly struck by a story about one of its most famous participants.

Anton Lang repeatedly played the role of Jesus to great acclaim. Between the first and second world wars he visited the United States and was saddened by the rise of groups preaching bigotry and violence.

"At Oberammergau" he told a reporter, "we have all kinds. There is a Catholic church, and a chapel that is used by the Protestants – Baptists, Methodists, Episcopalians and all kinds.

"But that isn't what counts. It is how one lives that makes one good or bad; and Jesus, I believe, will take us all to heaven according to our virtues."

It's only my humble opinion, but I think the casting directors made a very good choice when they selected Anton Lang for the role of Jesus.

# December

**READ** some words by a fourth-century Bishop of Constantinople and they reminded me of sitting on a grassy bank by the River Tweed, taking shelter from the flurrying snow on the ferry across the Mersey, lounging outside an ice-cream shop in Wales on the longest day, and chatting by the light of a wood fire in a bothy in the Galloway Hills.

What could John Chrysostom, who had never been within a thousand miles of any of those places, say to make me think of them?

"Such is friendship, that through it we love places and seasons; for as flowers drop their sweet leaves on the ground around them, so friends impart favour even to the places where they dwell."

The places we spend time with friends for ever retain, I think, traces of that friendship and become more special because of it.

Perhaps you would like to add some places of your own to that list.

## Saturday — December 2

**WAVING** her goodbye at the airport, John made the mistake of telling his youngest daughter he loved her with all his heart. His eldest daughter, who had come along to say goodbye to her sister, turned and mischievously commented, "You said you loved me with all your heart!"

"Well," John said, "I do!"

"And what about my brother?" she wanted to know. John assured her he also loved his son with all his heart.

"How is that even possible?" she asked.

"The heart is like Doctor Who's Tardis," he explained. "It's much bigger on the inside than it is on the outside!"

It might not be the most accurate or the most scientific explanation, I reflected when he told me about it. But it might come close to explaining the endless capability the heart has for giving "all" its love time after time, or several times at the same time.

157

## Sunday — December 3

IT is easy, in the longer, darker mornings or earlier nights, to lose things around the house. But the flick of a switch, or (in older days) the lighting of a candle, shows you that they were where they ought to be, or not far away from there, all along.

Sadly there are lives whose darkness isn't related to the cycle of the seasons; people who feel lost most days. Let us, you and me, be the candles that light their day, showing them that they aren't lost at all. Where they ought to be is often only a short walk away, a walk that will be shorter and more pleasant with some illuminating company.

How do you do that? Well, you light your candle or flick your switch and draw power from the One who is, and always has been, the Light of the World.

Then you take that light to where it might do most good.


## Monday — December 4

ROB was crossing a gorge by rope bridge in a game reserve in Mozambique. And it made him think!

It made him think how glad he was there was a net under the wooden planks he was stepping on. It made him think about how much he appreciated the modern materials it was made of. But it also made him think about the earlier builders of bridges just like the one swaying under his feet.

They made their ropes from grass! A few strands would be wound around each other and pulled tight. More strands would be added until they had a string. Those strings would be twisted around each other to make a rope. Ropes would be twisted until they had cables strong enough to take the weight of the people crossing.

"All from weak little strands of grass," he pointed out.

It reminded me that the little inconsequential decisions we make add up to bad or good days which, wrapped around each other, add up to wasted or productive weeks which, joined together, make meaningless or meaningful lives.

The bridge to the "other side" of life, like Rob's bridge across the gorge, is made up of lots of little things. Choose your "strands" well.

## Tuesday — December 5

WISDOM can often be found in the most unexpected of places. I recognised these words and a little stirring of the memory took me to a book of poems by Ella Wheeler Wilcox. Seven little words, but for the courage they would give and the good they might do they ought to be repeated around the world.

"Love lights more fires than hate extinguishes."

Imagine the fires we could light if we believed that, and the smouldering, dampened ashes we might reignite. Not real fires, of course, but hopes, dreams and aspirations – lit by love!

## Wednesday — December 6

AFTER decades of shuffling about the dance floor at weddings, Harry took the plunge and signed up for lessons. One particular couple always seemed in a hurry, bustling around the dance floor as if in a race. The teacher decided to have a word with the whole class.

"It's not about covering as much distance as you can," he said. "There is no particular place you need to reach. The whole point of dancing is simply to enjoy each step as you move around the floor."

"A good philosophy for the ballroom," Harry told me. "And, I dare say, an excellent philosophy for life."

I won't dance around it. He's right!

## Thursday — December 7

WE are into the Christmas month so I might be forgiven for asking – are you organised yet? I find a to-do list helps and a typical Christmas to-do list might go something like this.

*Buy presents. Wrap gifts. Send gifts. Shop for food. Make the food. See the lights.*

Now imagine writing that list with the spirit of Christmas in mind.

*Be present. Wrap someone in a hug. Send love. Share food. Make peace. Be the light.*

If you do both, then well done. But if you only have time for one list – make it the second one.

On, Prancer!

## Friday — December 8

*I LOVE the house at Christmas time,*
*The huge log fire, the Christmas tree,*
*But more than any other room*
*The kitchen is the place for me!*

*To step inside, and stamp the snow*
*From rubber boots, cheeks all aglow,*
*And toes and fingers feeling raw,*
*Then, gloriously, they start to thaw.*

*In warm, enveloping good cheer,*
*A warm mince-pie, a mug of tea,*
*With friends and family all around,*
*The kitchen is the place to be!*

*– Eileen Hay.*

## Saturday — December 9

IN Athens in 500 BC, young men had to graduate from the Ephebic College in order to become fully fledged citizens.

As part of their graduation they swore an oath, part of which declared, "I will not leave my country smaller when I die but greater and better, so far as I am able by myself and with the help of all."

A fine oath for a city state that seemed always to be at war – but an idea we might also take to heart in times of peace for our country, our town, our home, our family, our circle of friends, the needy in our neighbourhood . . .

In fact, no matter where we go or who we talk to we could do a lot worse than remember to leave the place better and the person happier for our having been there.

And, like those young Ancient Athenians, stepping up to take responsibility, we will generally find we don't have to do it on our own.

## Sunday — December 10

FLANNERY O'CONNOR, the American novelist, never wrote directly about faith, but her characters frequently had to deal with matters of religion as they affected their everyday lives.

A character of hers once spoke a line that surely came from Ms O'Connor's own attitude. It was, "I can, with one eye squinted, take it all as a blessing."

Whether everything in life is a blessing or not is surely a decision taken long ago up above. All we get to decide is whether we see it or not. Sometimes it's obvious, but sometimes we need to squint a little!

## Monday — December 11

BANKS will try to attract us and our money by offering a good rate of return. They promise we will (eventually) get more money back than we put in. That's a fine thought – but the 19th-century writer John Ruskin had a finer one.

"Give a little love to a child," he wrote, "and you get a great deal back."

Love is surely the ingredient that unlocks the potential in each of us. Giving it to a child is the best way of making sure they become all the good things they might be. That's a rate of return that isn't just good for our personal account; it's good for the whole world.

## Tuesday — December 12

CRAIG is very aware that people abuse the service of his food bank. He doesn't like it, but he doesn't let it interfere with the good work being done.

"If accepting that we are going to be taken advantage of by some is the price we have to pay to help others, then that's fine," he says.

My thoughts immediately went to an old African proverb.

"If you close your eyes to the bad people around you," it reminds us, "you will also not see the good people passing by."

## Wednesday — December 13

THERE'S a man who stands in the shallows of Loch Earn all year round. Actually "he" is a mirrored metal sculpture of a man. Created by Rob Mulholland and called Still, but known as the Mirror Man, he was installed there to reflect the beauty all around him.

He is a fine piece of artwork in his own right, but it's the reflection of beauty that makes him stand out from other statues.

So, would we benefit from spending more of our lives reflecting the good and the beauty in the world? I think we would. But I'd recommend finding somewhere drier and warmer to stand.

## Thursday — December 14

BELIEVE it or not, the great actress Katharine Hepburn learned an important life lesson from a bar of soap. Her father, she said, usually had one bar of good soap by his sink. He used it for cleaning himself and other things, washing his hair, shaving and brushing his teeth. It was simple, economical and an example of how to live an "uncluttered" life.

In her own uncluttered life she focused on a few friends, her family and her work (with undeniably excellent results).

I guess we could all benefit from uncluttering our lives – but I draw the line at brushing my teeth with soap!

## Friday — December 15

THE story goes that research experts discovered a "drug" that has the potential to be a worldwide best-selling product because of the beneficial effects it has.

But the experts won't be making any money, because the product can't be packaged or sold. What was it?

Gratitude! Apparently the more we are thankful for, the more we will have to be thankful for, not just emotionally, but physically as well.

It might or might not be true – but I'll be grateful for the opportunity to find out!

## Saturday — December 16

A LOT of people feel the pressure to be perfect. The expectations they have and the standards they set for themselves can lead to all sorts of problems. But let me take you on a short trip to Turkey!

The skill of Turkish carpet weavers is recognised all over the world, but even the best of their carpets or rugs will be imperfect by design. You see, they have a tradition of weaving a mistake into the pattern somewhere because perfection, they believe, belongs only to God.

## Sunday — December 17

A LBERT EINSTEIN understood the structure of the universe. He also understood that nothing he could do would ever alter it.

But there was something he could play a part in changing.

"Maybe, by raising my voice," he said, "I can help the greatest of all causes – goodwill among men and peace on earth."

We don't have to be Einstein to understand how worthwhile that would be. May we all play our part in the cause – even if only in our own homes – and may we all get to share in that peace and goodwill that comes about because of it.

## Monday — December 18

THE Scots missionary Mary Slessor described this trait – or perhaps it's a talent – as, "Undefinable, untranslatable, and yet the most real thing and the greatest power in human life. The man or woman who possesses this subtle gift possesses the most precious thing on earth."

Wow! What wonderful thing was she referring to? And who wouldn't want to be rich in it, whatever it was?

It wasn't one of the usual suspects like love or faith. It was sympathy! Not just the kind that leaves us feeling sorry for others as we go about our own business, but the kind that helps us understand their difficulties and moves us to help our brother or sister.

With enough of that "subtle gift" we might change the world in a not-so-subtle way.

Golden glow.

## Tuesday — December 19

SOMETIMES people reach a point in their lives where they stop learning; they decide (without really thinking about it) that they know all they need to know.

As an approach to life it has the benefit of simplicity, I suppose, but I can't help thinking a lot gets missed out that way.

A life of learning and wonder and delight is possible. We don't need to reach a certain point and stop. So, you might ask, how do we do that? Well, we could do worse than learn from a great philosopher who took his lesson, in turn, from the natural world.

The German writer and thinker Johann Wolfgang von Goethe once observed, "Nature is whole, and yet she is never finished."

Nature is also much, much older than any of us, and yet she still has time for buttercups and rainbows. We should consider ourselves whole at whatever age we might be, but always have space in our hearts for a new season.

## Wednesday — December 20

THERE are many words of wisdom attributed to the "Indians" of the old west. Some are authentic, some less so, but there is often a core of truth there regardless of the provenance.

The Lakota chief, Sitting Bull, was asked why he was so loved and respected by his people. In response Sitting Bull asked if it was true that the leader of the white folk – the President – was respected because he had "many horses and many houses."

On being assured it was true, Sitting Bull shook his head and said his people loved and respected him because he kept nothing for himself.

Jesus said to sell our possessions and give the money to the poor. Other words of wisdom say that what you give away will come back to you. Sitting Bull gave his "horses and houses" to his people and in return they made him their chief.

Let's be known for what we give rather than for what we receive. And let's stand by ready to be amazed by the consequences.

## Thursday — December 21

THE environmentalist Edward Abbey once wrote, "May your trails be crooked, lonesome, winding and dangerous, leading to the most amazing views. May your mountains rise into and above the clouds." The first time I read it I took it as meaning that the things worth achieving were often difficult; the out-of-the-way path leads to the best view; the best way to see the clouds is to rise above them.

Then a friend sent me a picture of the Path to Heaven. The photographer captured a beautiful sunrise above an ordinary grassy hill. The path up that hill and into the sunrise looked like it might have been worn away by quad bikes and walkers.

The fact that this muddy path looked like many I had walked comforted me with the thought that I might well be able to navigate my way to the destination (with a little effort and a bit of faith).

Be they muddy like in the photo, or winding and cloudy like in the quote from Abbey, the paths we walk to Heaven (along with our Heavenly Guide) won't be marble staircases like in a Busby Berkeley Hollywood spectacular. They will be recognisable to each of us, because we will walk them, overcome their challenges and become better people because of them, day-by-day in our ordinary lives.

## Friday — December 22

THE temptation at Christmas to put on a good spread, to buy the best presents and have the prettiest decorations is understandable and not a bad thing. After all, you are doing the best you can for your guests and that's kind of you.

There is an Albanian Christmas tradition that allows for all of those things – but they also spread some hay under the dinner table. Just as a reminder of the humble situation the Lord was born into.

So, by all means celebrate Christmas in the grand style. But find a space in it all for a little humility, a little unnoticed kindness, a little charity.

Jesus will be with any loving family gathered around the table in his name, but he will also be with the needy and desperate. This year, try to find him in both of those places.

## Saturday — December 23

THEY say the whole notion of a white Christmas came about because it snowed on the first eight Christmases of Charles Dickens's life. So, when he wrote "A Christmas Carol", naturally he set it in snow.

Such can be the humble beginnings of great traditions. And each of us has the opportunity to continue one or create one this Christmas. Let's make it something beautiful; something, like a white Christmas, worth hoping for and getting excited about.

## Sunday — December 24

THE "Love" verses from Corinthians are amongst the most famous lines in the Good Book. But allow me, please, to offer up this extract from Christmas Corinthians by someone whose name I do not know, but whose heart I feel I know well.

"If I decorate my house perfectly with plaid bows and strands of twinkling lights, but do not show love, I'm just another decorator.

If I work at the soup kitchen, carol in the nursing home and give all that I have to charity, but do not show love, it profits me nothing.

If I trim the spruce with shimmering angels and crocheted snowflakes, attend myriad holiday parties and sing in the choir's cantata but do not focus on Christ, I have missed the point.

Love stops the cooking to hug the child. Love sets aside the decorating to kiss the husband. Love is kind, though tired.

Love doesn't envy another's home that has co-ordinated Christmas china and table linens. Love doesn't yell at the kids to get out of the way, but is thankful they are there to be in the way.

Love doesn't give only to those who are able to give in return but rejoices in giving to those who can't.

Love bears all things, believes all things, hopes all things, endures all things. Love never fails.

Video games will break, pearl necklaces will be lost, golf clubs will rust, but giving the gift of love will endure."

As the poet Christina Rossetti pointed out, "Love came down at Christmas."

## Monday — December 25

ARTABAN, the Other Wise Man in the story by Henry van Dyke, set out for Bethlehem after the Magi.

Always running late, he missed the baby Jesus, but he spent the next thirty years using the treasures he brought for the baby to help others.

Eventually, feeling he had failed in his quest, he had a vision. Jesus himself assured Artaban that every time he helped someone he had actually been in the presence of his Lord.

That is something worth remembering as we give and receive our gifts this Christmas.

## Tuesday — December 26

FRIENDS who have been to Helsinki tell me about the Kamppi Chapel of Silence.

From the outside it looks like the rounded prow of a ship made from narrow horizontal strips of laminated and varnished pine.

Run by various church parishes and the city's social services, it's designed not for services but as a refuge; a place of peace in the bustling city.

It features high on the list of things to do in Helsinki. Mostly, I suspect, because the people who have already been there have felt the wonder of peace in an unexpected place.

It's like the legend of the king who asked his artists to paint a picture of peace. They mostly came up with images of tranquil valleys, families walking hand in hand, ducks on still millponds . . .

The winner painted a scene of battle under thunderclouds. But one patch of sky was blue, and in it, unaffected by the noise and the anger, flew a white dove.

Peace and silence might be found almost anywhere, but they are only truly appreciated in the midst of their opposites.

The Kamppi Chapel is the equivalent of that painted bird for the people of Helsinki. May Boxing Day be your dove after the the hustle and bustle of Christmas – should you need it.

## Wednesday — December 27

PHILLIPS BROOKS was the clergyman who wrote the Christmas hymn "O Little Town Of Bethlehem".

As well as those beautiful words, he offered the world these – "Be such a person and live such a life that if everyone were such as you and every life such as yours this Earth would be God's Paradise."

A question worth asking is, "If everyone behaved and believed like me, would I like the world that came to be because of it?"

If the answer is yes then you are obviously doing fine. If the answer is no then set about making it so!

## Thursday — December 28

AS President of the United States, Woodrow Wilson knew a thing or two about power, and he tried to share that knowledge with the graduating students of Swarthmore College.

"Do you covet honor?" he asked. "You never will get it by serving yourself. Do you covet distinction? You will only get it as the servant of mankind. Do not forget why you are here. You are here in order to enable the world to live more amply, with greater vision, with a finer spirit of hope and achievement. You are here to enrich the world – and you impoverish yourself if you forget the errand."

We might forget many an errand in our time. May we always remember this one!

## Friday — December 29

WAR AND PEACE". That was the epic novel by Tolstoy, wasn't it? But I was thinking of a shorter work on the same themes by Benjamin Franklin which might have "epic" consequences.

He suggested, "Be at war with your vices, at peace with your neighbours, and let every New Year find you a better man."

Regardless of the success or otherwise of our other resolutions, and regardless of how good we may have been, let us strive always to be simply better than we were.

## Saturday — December 30

*A*LTHOUGH *I'd heard gyms could be useful,*
   *Till lately, I'd never attended.*
*I'm so glad I've taken the plunge, though –*
*For, oh, goodness me, it is splendid!*
*So, here's what I do: there's a big pool,*
*Like a beautiful, shimmering lake.*
*And after I've swum a whole length – well!*
*I feel I deserve a nice cake.*
*I then meet my friend in the café*
*('Gym buddy', I think is the phrase).*
*We always select the fruit option –*
*Like gateau with blueberry glaze.*
*We then retire to the Jacuzzi*
*Or sauna – it's tricky to choose –*
*Then back to the pool (well, the loungers –*
*A lovely, warm spot for a snooze.)*
*And every so often we wonder,*
*Do we use the gym as we should?*
*I feel that there's something we're missing –*
*But I'm certain it's doing us good!*

                                      – Emma Canning.

## Sunday — December 31

NO-ONE really knows why Scots refer to the last day of the year as Hogmanay, although the whole world knows how well they celebrate it! One of the theories relates to the Auld Alliance with France and the time when New Year was a more prominent celebration than Christmas. But, even then, Christ was still there.

A French song sung at the time began with the words "Homme est né" (Hom-eh-nay.) which translates as "The man is born." The song has to do with Christmas and the visit of the three kings, but the name seems to have become attached to New Year's Eve. Perhaps because that birth also represented a new beginning.

At the end of the old year, as at the beginning of the new, "Homme est né" or "Hogmanay" reminds us that Jesus is the Alpha and the Omega, the beginning and the end.

Have a happy 2018!

Perfect trust.

# Chris Riddell

1. Lives by the Seaside in Brighton with his wife and three children.

2. Writes and illustrates books like these by himself ⟶

   The Emperor of Absurdia | Wendel's Workshop | Ottoline and the Yellow Cat | Ottoline goes to School

   and books like these with Paul Stewart. ⟶

   The Blobheads | MUDDLE EARTH | THE EDGE CHRONICLES

3. Draws a cartoon every Sunday for the Observer newspaper.

4. Has two of these in a box where he keeps his treasures ⟶

   KATE GREENAWAY MEDAL    KATE GREENAWAY MEDAL

   and four of these on his son Jack's bookshelf. ⟶

   | SMARTIES GOLD AWARD | NESTLÉ SILVER AWARD | NESTLÉ SILVER AWARD | NESTLÉ SILVER AWARD |
   |---|---|---|---|
   | FOR FERGUS CRANE | FOR CORBY FLOOD | FOR HUGO PEPPER | FOR THE EMPEROR OF ABSURDIA |

5. His first school blazer was black with green ribbon and made him feel very uncomfortable ⟶
   (if you'd like to know more, visit www.panmacmillan.com/chrisriddell)

# THE Ottoline Books

NESTLÉ CHILDREN'S BOOK PRIZE GOLD MEDAL

WINNER SHEFFIELD CHILDREN'S BOOK AWARD
SHORTER NOVELS CATEGORY

WINNER RED HOUSE CHILDREN'S BOOK AWARD FOR YOUNGER READERS

WINNER LINCOLNSHIRE YOUNG PEOPLE'S BOOK AWARD

WINNER HIGHLAND CHILDREN'S BOOK AWARD

SHORTLISTED FOR THE CILIP KATE GREENAWAY MEDAL

BIG CITY LITERARY GOBLET FOR BOOKS ABOUT HAIRY NORWEGIAN BOG PEOPLE

QUOTES

'Beautifully illustrated'
*Guardian*

'Each page is designed with retro elegance'
*Sunday Times*

Look out for more adventures
with OTTOLINE

Ottoline and the Yellow Cat

Ottoline at Sea

# Chris RIDDELL

# Ottoline
## goes to
# School

MACMILLAN CHILDREN'S BOOKS

For my sister, Lynn

# Chapter One

Ottoline lived in Apartment 243 of the P. W. HUFFLEDINCK TOWER, which everybody called the Pepperpot Building because it looked like one.

THE PEPPERPOT BUILDING

THE POINTY TOWER

APARTMENT 243

THE SHOEBOX BUILDING

THE ICE-CREAM CONE BUILDING

Ottoline
LIKES SOLVING TRICKY PROBLEMS AND WORKING OUT CLEVER PLANS IN HER NOTEBOOK

PETTIGREW PARK AND ORNAMENTAL GARDENS

Her parents were Collectors who travelled around the world. They were hardly ever at home, but Ottoline was well looked after and she was never lonely. And besides, she had her best friend, Mr. Munroe, for company.

Jean-Pierre

FROM THE HOME-COOKED MEAL Co

Pete

FROM McBEAN'S CLEANING SERVICE

Kate and Teresa

FROM SMITH & SMITH PILLOW-PLUMPING AND CURTAIN-DRAWING TECHNICIANS

Madame Wong

FROM THE SMILING DRAGON CLOTHES-FOLDING Co

Geraldine and Geraldine

FROM HAPPY NEST BED MAKERS

Marion

FROM MARIONS BATHROOM SUPPLIES

Mr. Munroe

FROM NORWAY

Big Doug

FROM DOOR-HANDLE SHINERS INC.

The Guys

FROM THE 1,000-STRONG LIGHTBULB CHANGING Co

Although Ottoline's parents were away a lot, they always kept in touch with postcards.

Greetings from the
NOME ELK-DECORATING FESTIVAL

POSTCARD

Dearest O,
    Decorating
Elks is great fun
but very tiring!
Pa sends his love,
    lots of love,
        Ma.
P.S. Be careful on
those swings!
    X X X

NORTH WOODS
22·2·08

22¢

Miss O. Brown,
Apt. 243,
The Pepperpot Bld.
3rd Street,
BIG CITY 3001

OTTOLINE WRITES TO HER PARENTS
BY SENDING LETTERS TO THE
ROVING COLLECTORS' SOCIETY.
THEY MAKE SURE ROVING COLLECTORS
GET THEIR POST NO MATTER WHERE
IN THE WORLD THEY HAPPEN TO BE.

MONDAY
SUNGLASSES

TUESDAY
COAT

WEDNESDAY
DUNGAREES

THURSDAY
EAR MUFFS

FRIDAY
JUMPER

FRIDAY

SATURDAY
SUN HAT

SUNDAY
SILLY GLASSES

(INDOORS
ONLY)

OTTOLINE WAS
WEARING HER
TUESDAY COAT.
SHE HAD A SPECIAL
ITEM OF CLOTHING
FOR EACH DAY
OF THE WEEK

One morning Ottoline and Mr. Munroe
were taking a walk in Pettigrew Park and
Ornamental Gardens. It was a Tuesday, and
on Tuesday mornings they liked to visit the
turtles in the Turtle Pool . . .

. . . which is where they met Cecily Forbes-Lawrence III and her Patagonian pony, Mumbles.

EAST CROYDON
MARSHMALLOW TREE

NORFOLK
SNAFFLER

EAST AFRICAN
TUFTY SHRUB

"I like your pony," said Ottoline.

"Thank you," said Cecily. "Mumbles is from Patagonia, you know. I like your dog."

"That's not a dog," laughed Ottoline. "That's Mr. Munroe."

Ottoline and Cecily fed the turtles stale
crackers that Mr. Munroe had brought
especially, and Cecily told Ottoline a
fascinating story about a boy with
feet so enormous that he could
use them as a sunshade.

THE BOY WITH ENORMOUS FEET

"... and then Rupert became the world junior hopscotch champion, but that's another story," said Cecily. "I must go now. Mumbles's mane needs brushing."

"Can I help?" asked Ottoline excitedly. She loved brushing hair. Mr. Munroe didn't.

"Maybe some other time," said Cecily, walking off in the direction of the ornamental maze. "By the way, your dog's coat needs brushing too."

"She seems nice," said Ottoline, after Cecily had gone. Mr. Munroe didn't say anything.

The next day Ottoline met Cecily on the ornamental bridge.

They played Pooh Sticks with twigs that Mr. Munroe had found especially.

Cecily told Ottoline all about her Great-Uncle Oscar, the misunderstood pirate.

OSCAR THE MISUNDERSTOOD PIRATE

". . . and in the end he had four parrots, two on each shoulder, but they were no help when his trousers caught fire, but that's another story," said Cecily. "I must go now. I've got to take Mumbles to his showjumping class."

"Can I watch?" asked Ottoline excitedly. Mr. Munroe didn't have any classes. He was too shy.

"Maybe some other time," said Cecily, walking off in the direction of the bonsai-tree forest. "Your dog's dropped your umbrella."

"I like her," said Ottoline after Cecily had gone. "She tells amazing stories."

Mr. Munroe didn't hear her. He was busy fishing the umbrella out of the ornamental stream.

He got very wet.

The next day Ottoline met Cecily
in the park . . .

. . . and the next day . . .

. . . and the next.

"… and all they found was a skeleton wearing a blue polka-dot bow tie," said Cecily.

"Incredible," said Ottoline. "I must go now. Mr. Munroe doesn't like the rain, and it's almost teatime."

"Can I come?" asked Cecily.

"Of course you can, Cecily," said Ottoline excitedly. "Mr. Munroe and I would like that very much, wouldn't we, Mr. Munroe?"

Mr. Munroe didn't say anything.

Ottoline didn't notice. She was busy catching up with Cecily, who was walking off in the direction of the Pepperpot Building.

# Chapter Two

Ottoline and Cecily had tea on the Beidermeyer sofa.

Cecily told Ottoline about her family. Her father was somebody extremely important in the Big City Bank. He had meetings all day long, and when he came home he would have more meetings about the meetings he was going to have the next day. His secretary was called Miss Hopkins and she arranged his meetings.

MISS HOPKINS

MUMBLES HAD
A SAUCER OF
MILK

CECILY PUT A
SAUCER DOWN
FOR MR. MUNROE

If Cecily wanted her father to read her a bedtime story she had to arrange it with Miss Hopkins well in advance, so usually she didn't bother.

OTTOLINE WAS VERY IMPRESSED WITH THE WAY CECILY SIPPED HER TEA

A DOUBLE-SPOUTED TEAPOT FROM OTTOLINE'S PARENTS' TEAPOT COLLECTION

Cecily's mother was somebody extremely important in the Big City Museum of Modern Art. She went to parties almost every night. When she wasn't going to other people's parties she was having parties of her own. Her secretary was called Miss Dickinson and she arranged her parties. If Cecily wanted her mother to tuck her up in bed she had to arrange it with Miss Dickinson well in advance, so usually she didn't bother.

MISS DICKINSON

". . . of course, I'm fine about it," said Cecily. "But it's Mumbles I feel sorry for. Mother and Father are just too busy to take any notice of him, and Patagonian ponies can be very sensitive, you know."

"Can they? How fascinating," said Ottoline, pouring them another cup. "We should do this more often."

"I'm afraid I can't," said Cecily. "Mumbles and I have to go back to school next week."

"School?" said Ottoline.

"Yes," said Cecily. "The Alice B. Smith School for the Differently Gifted."

"It sounds like fun," said Ottoline.

"It isn't," said Cecily firmly. "By the way, where has your dog got to?"

Mr. Munroe was up on the roof of the
Pepperpot Building, which is where he often
went when he was sad. Ottoline was his best
friend and he didn't want to share her.

Ever since Professor and Professor Brown had found him in a bog in Norway and brought him back to live with them, Mr. Munroe and Ottoline had been inseparable.

They had had all sorts of adventures together . . .

Like the time they found
themselves at sea . . .

YOU CAN
READ ALL ABOUT
IT IN "OTTOLINE
AT SEA"

. . . and the time they caught the notorious
jewel thief the Yellow Cat . . .

YOU CAN
READ ALL ABOUT
IT IN "OTTOLINE
AND THE YELLOW CAT"

But that's another story.

The sun came out and a warm breeze ruffled Mr. Munroe's hair. The sun didn't come out very often in the bog in Norway. It felt good to be standing on the roof of the Pepperpot Building instead of in a wet puddle in a cold bog. It felt good to have Ottoline as his best friend, and Cecily wasn't so bad. Not really.

When Mr. Munroe came down from the roof Cecily and Mumbles had gone.

"Feeling better?" Ottoline asked.

Mr. Munroe nodded.

"Good," said Ottoline. "I've got a clever plan!"

Mr. Munroe sat on the Beidermeyer rocking chair with a little sigh.

"I've just asked Ma and Pa to send us to school!"

BY CARRIER PIGEON

Professor & Professor
Brown
c/o The Roving Collectors'
Society

Dear Ma and Pa,
I think it is time for me to go to a proper school. My new friend Cecily Forbes-Lawrence III goes to the Alice B. Smith School for the Differently Gifted and is very good at sipping tea. Mr. Munroe and I would like to discover our different gifts so we can help you in your collecting when we grow up,

lots of love,

P.S. I'm giving this letter to Max to deliver to the society on his paper round. Write back soon!

○
xxx

OTTOLINE'S LETTER TO HER PARENTS

# Chapter Three

Two days later, Mr. Munroe found a postcard and a brown-paper parcel on the doormat.

Greetings From the Sarawak Hornbill Festival

POSTCARD

Dearest O,
          I'm so pleased you've decided that you'd like to go to school. We've contacted the Alice B. Smith School and they were delighted to accept you.
Pa sends his love,
          lots of love,
                    Ma.
P.S. Your suitcase is in the cupboard. XXX

RAIN FOREST
13·04·08

86¢

Miss O Brown,
Apt. 243,
The Pepperpot Bld,
3rd Street,
BIG CITY 3001

Mr. Munroe took the
postcard and the brown-paper
parcel to Ottoline, who was
busy arranging her Odd Shoe
collection.

34

WHENEVER
OTTOLINE BUYS
SHOES, SHE WEARS
ONE AND ADDS THE
OTHER TO HER ODD
SHOE COLLECTION

Ottoline read the postcard and then opened
the brown-paper parcel.

HAT

GYMSLIP

BLAZER

35

THESE WERE
IN THE PARCEL

TIE

SHIRTS

APRON

PYJAMAS

UNDERWEAR

MR. MUNROE KEPT
THE STRING TO ADD
TO THE BALL OF
STRING IN HIS
BEDROOM

"Thank you, Mr. Munroe,"
she said. "We must pack
straight away!"

When Ottoline opened the cupboard to get her suitcase, a large bear stepped out.

EXTREMELY
SMALL
PAINTING

OLD
CURTAINS

"Hello," said Ottoline to the bear. "Would you mind handing me my suitcase?"

"Not at all," said the bear, rummaging in the cupboard. "Going somewhere nice?"

"I'm going to the Alice B. Smith School for the Differently Gifted!" said Ottoline with a big smile. "You can help me pack if you like."

"I'd be delighted," said the bear. "And I'll look after the apartment while you're away — I'm sure there's snow on the way."

THE BEAR HAD NEVER BEEN TO SCHOOL, BUT HE SEEMED TO KNOW EXACTLY WHAT TO PACK

39

THE PICNIC CLUB
IN THE WOODS
Admit one + a friend
FROM MIDNIGHT TILL LATE    BLACK TIE

THE BEAR WAS EXTREMELY WELL TRAVELLED SO WAS VERY GOOD AT PACKING SUITCASES

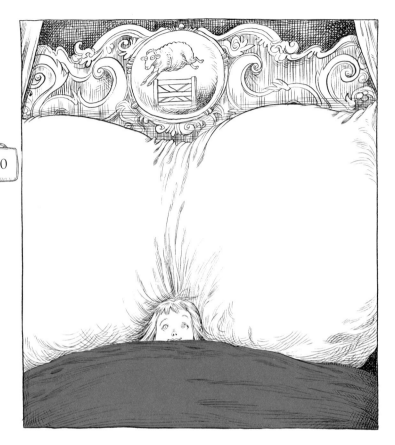

That night Ottoline was so excited she
couldn't sleep. She had never been to school.
Instead she did the lessons her mother and
father, Professor and Professor Brown, sent
her every week.

Sometimes they were hard . . .

Sometimes they were complicated . . .

And sometimes . . .

↑ THIS WAY UP ↑

. . . they were fun.

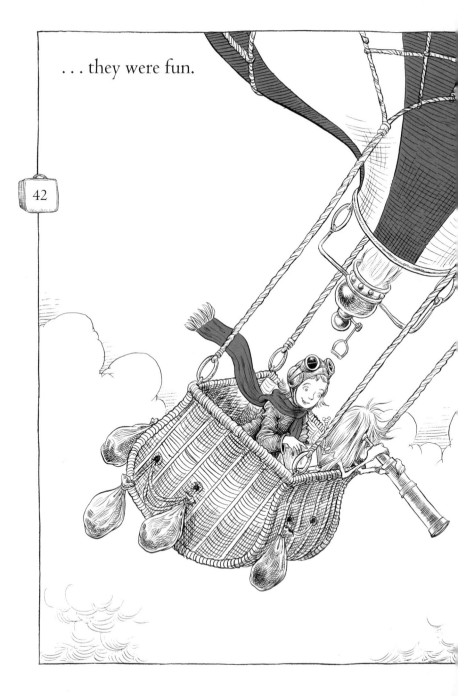

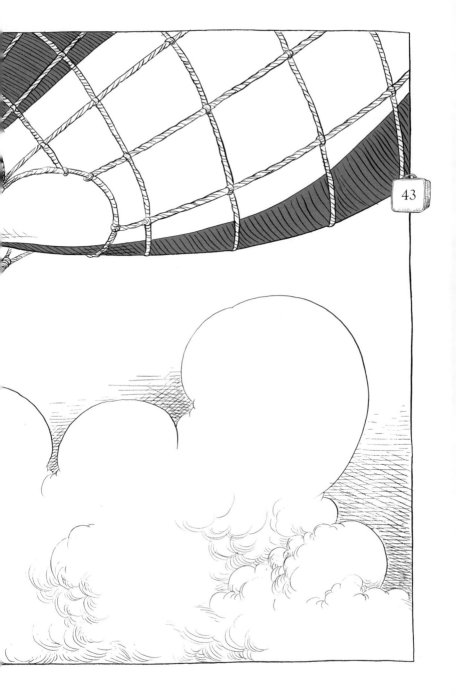

Although Ottoline had lots of friends in the Big City . . .

THE BEAR FROM THE BASEMENT

VIVIENNE FROM THE 3rd ST SHOE STORE

MRS. PASTERNAK FROM APARTMENT 244 AND HER PET MONKEY, MORRIS

MAX THE PAPER BOY

MR. MUNROE

. . . she had never been to school, so she didn't have any school friends.

Ottoline couldn't wait to go to the Alice B. Smith School for the Differently Gifted with her new friend Cecily, which was why she was too excited to sleep.

Mr. Munroe didn't sleep much either.

# Chapter Four

I n the morning, Ottoline and Mr. Munroe said goodbye to the bear and walked to the bus stop on the corner of 3rd Street and Windmill.

A yellow school bus drew up.

"You must be Ottoline Brown," said the driver. "Hop in."

Ottoline climbed on to the yellow school bus. "Welcome aboard," said the driver. "I'm Alice B. Smith, and these are my gifted students." Alice B. Smith introduced everyone to Ottoline. There was Brian, the son of the Invisible Man, and his dog, Bodge. Then the Wright sisters, Orvillise and Wilburta, and their toucan, Richard. Behind them sat the Sultana of Pahang and her hairy elephant, Bye-Bye, and Ottoline's new friend Cecily with Mumbles the pony. At the back sat Newton Knight the Boy Genius and his robot, Skittles.

Ottoline sat down next to Cecily and the
school bus rattled and shuddered as it set off
through the city.

"Have I ever told you about the time I
caught a mermaid?" said Cecily.

"I don't think so," said Ottoline, "but it
sounds fascinating."

They left Big City and drove high into the mountains.

53

Eventually they came to a large mansion on top of a mountain.

The door of the mansion was opened by an extremely tall butler.

"Well, here we are. Home sweet home!" said Alice B. Smith with a smile. "Solihull will show you to your rooms. Sleep well – school begins tomorrow at thirteen o'clock sharp."

They all followed Solihull the butler up an extremely grand staircase. On the wall were pictures of famous ex-pupils of the Alice B. Smith School for the Differently Gifted.

THE NABOB OF SOB

BALDY McSTEWART, THE FRIDGE MAGNATE

DOTTIE NEUWORTH, THE OPERATIC YODELLER

60

THE
INVISIBLE
MAN

MICHAEL
MOUSE

61

Solihull showed the pupils to their rooms.

"Your dog has to go with the other pets," said Cecily. "They sleep in the East Wing."

"See you in the morning," said Ottoline to Mr. Munroe.

63

BY HOT AIR BALLOON

Professor & Professor
Brown
c/o The Roving Collectors
Society

Dear Ma and Pa,

I'm sharing a room with my friend Cecily Forbes-Lawrence III. Her grandmother is called Cecily Forbes-Lawrence I and was an extremely famous opera singer. I haven't discovered my different gift yet,

lots of love,

65

X X X.

P.S. I'm giving this letter to Solihull the butler to deliver to the Society when he does the shopping. Write back soon!

P.P.S. Cecily didn't sleep well. She is worried about Mumbles. She says he is homesick.

# Chapter Five

The next morning at thirteen o'clock Alice B. Smith showed the pupils the timetable . . .

THE SCHOOL CLOCK

ALICE B. SMITH THINKS DRESSING UP IS VERY IMPORTANT AND THAT THE NUMBER NINE IS UNLUCKY. SHE DOESN'T BELIEVE IN WEDNESDAYS

| | MONDAY | TUESDAY | THURSDAY | FRIDAY | THE WEEKEND |
|---|---|---|---|---|---|
| **L E S S O N 1** | SITTING PRACTICE | LOOKING | GIGGLING STUDIES | USEFUL SKILLS | **P E R S O N A L   D E V E L O P M E N T** |
| **L E S S O N 2** | PAPER FOLDING | SEEMING | WEEPING WORKSHOP | USELESS SKILLS | |
| **T H E   A F T E R N O O N** | LUNCH | PICNIC | BUNFIGHT | BANQUET | |
| | ADVANCED MUSING | BEING | TEACUP CLASS | WHISTLING CHOIR | |
| **E V E N I N G** | FREE TIME | | | | |
| | BEDTIME | | | | |

. . . and the lessons began.

67

# MONDAY

## SITTING PRACTICE

CORRECT POSTURE WHEN SITTING ON AN OTTOMAN

## PAPER FOLDING

THE FIVE-FOLD PARTY INVITATION

68

## LUNCH

SOMETHING BROWN AND STRINGY

SOMETHING GREEN AND MUSHY

SOMETHING YELLOW AND LUMPY

## ADVANCED MUSING

THINKING ABOUT CLOUDS

OTTOLINE'S NOTEBOOK

Strange noises in the night - MUST INVESTIGATE...

Brian the invisible boy without his clothes!

Advanced Musing is VERY HARD, I think!

# TUESDAY

LOOKING

EAGLE
SPOTTING

70

IMPERSONATING
A HEDGE

SEEMING

BEING

BEING
A
PRINCESS

PICNIC

SOLIHULL'S JAM AND
FISH PASTE SANDWICHES

OTTOLINE'S
NOTEBOOK

Mr. Munroe thinks my
different gift looks
like this and he is
looking for
it all over
the school!!

Cecily is very good
at being a princess.

WOOF!

71

# FRIDAY

## USEFUL SKILLS

CONKERS

## USELESS SKILLS

BURP!

74

## BANQUET

← SOLIHULL'S BANGERS AND MASH

## WHISTLING CHOIR

TWINKLE, TWINKLE, LITTLE STAR

Newton Knight the cleverest b
in the world, b
I'm better at
burping!
Cecily says
Mumbles is still
homesick.

OTTOLINE'S
NOTEBOOK

75

On Friday night, Ottoline visited Mr. Munroe in the East Wing.

"I've had such a busy week!" she told him. "Looking lessons and teacup class and paper folding and whistling . . ."

Mr. Munroe had had a busy week too, searching for Ottoline's Different Gift, which he was sure must be somewhere in the school. He had been looking for it that morning when he saw Mumbles the Patagonian pony disappear down a long corridor. Mr. Munroe was about to tell Ottoline this when Cecily interrupted them.

"I hate weekends," complained Cecily. "At weekends we have 'Personal Development'."

"What's that?" asked Ottoline.

"You'll see," said Cecily, "but first you're invited to my slumber party tonight." Cecily looked at Mr. Munroe. "Dogs aren't allowed," she said.

# Chapter Six

That night Cecily hosted the slumber party in her five-poster bed.

"You have the nicest room," said Wilburta.

"I know," said Cecily casually, "but I prefer my bedroom at home. It's much bigger . . ." Cecily examined her fingernails. "And besides," she went on, "my bedroom at home isn't haunted."

"Haunted?" everybody exclaimed at once. "The Alice B. Smith School is haunted?"

"Yes," said Cecily with a yawn. "Didn't you know? Once upon a time," she began, "there was a pretty young teacher called Alice Brunhilda Smith, who was best friends with a beautiful opera singer called Cecily. She played piano for Cecily and helped her learn her lines, until Cecily became famous and married a cod-liver-oil tycoon whose brother was a notorious pirate, but that's another story . . .

79

"Anyway, Alice decided to look for another challenge and set off in her Armstrong-Siddley three-wheeler.

"One dark and stormy Wednesday night the Armstrong-Siddley broke down on a lonely mountain road miles from anywhere . . ."

"I'm frightened," said Orvillise.

"Go on," said Ottoline in a whisper.

"Well," said Cecily, "Alice saw a light in the distance and decided to go and ask for help.

"Alice knocked on the front door and waited.
There was the sound of great heavy footsteps
approaching, the jangling of keys and then
a long creaking squeak as the door slowly
opened . . ."

"I'm frightened," said Wilburta.
"Go on," said Ottoline in a whisper.

"Standing there was a young man with big, clunky shoes and rather wild hair. 'Hello,' he said. 'Welcome to Hammerstein Castle. My name is Hector Hammerstein. How can I help you?'

"'My car has broken down,' said Alice. 'I don't suppose . . .'

"'Leave it to me,' said Hector. 'I'll have Solihull bring it to my laboratory.'

"Just then there was a jagged flash of lightning and a tremendous clap of thunder and a huge monster appeared in the doorway.

"Hector Hammerstein told Alice not to be frightened. The monster's name was Solihull and he was the butler. He'd been created in the laboratory by Hector's father, the mad scientist Dudley Hammerstein. Solihull was very good-natured, Hector explained, and he kept the mansion spick and span. The only frightening thing about Solihull was his love of jam and fish paste sandwiches."

"What about the ghost?" asked the Sultana of Pahang.

"I was just getting to that," said Cecily. "Solihull brought the car to the laboratory and Hector set about fixing it. It took quite some time, but Alice was very impressed.

"'I'm very impressed, Hector,' she said when he'd finished. 'I think you've found your gift . . .' Just then, the clock struck nine o'clock . . ."

I'M FINDING THIS STORY RATHER UNSETTLING...
I'M FRIGHTENED!
I'M SCARED

AND ALL THE LIGHTS WENT OUT...

87

ME TOO!

AND ME...

WHAT HAPPENED NEXT, CECILY?

"When the lights came back on, Alice's car was a wreck. It had been battered and pulverized and was covered in horseshoe-shaped dents.

"'It's the curse of the Horse of the Hammersteins!' exclaimed Hector, turning pale and trembling. 'My father got rid of the family carriage and replaced it with a luxury limousine. The family horse never forgave him. Although it went on to have a very successful career in carriage croquet, it vowed to return and haunt the castle in revenge!'

"'How fascinating,' said Alice.

"'This is the final straw. I've had enough!' said Hector. 'I'm just not cut out to be a mad scientist. I've done the hair and the clunky shoes, but my heart just isn't in it. You can have the mansion. I'm off to Big City for a quiet life!'

"So Hector left and started the extremely successful Hammerstein's Horseless Carriage Repairs Co., and Alice stayed and started her School for the Differently Gifted," said Cecily.

"But on dark, stormy nights, the Horse of the Hammersteins returns to seek revenge for the terrible wrong it suffered, by scaring anyone it finds out of their wits, or worse . . ."

"Worse?" said Wilburta, Orvillise, Brian, Newton and the Sultana of Pahang.

"Time for bed," Cecily yawned.

Everybody went to bed . . .

. . . but nobody slept well . . .

THE FORBES-LAWRENCE
ROOM

SOB

. . . except for Ottoline.

93

# Chapter Seven

"Here at the Alice B. Smith School for the Differently Gifted," said Alice B. Smith the next morning, "we like to encourage our pupils to develop their different gifts."

"Excuse me, Miss Smith," said Ottoline, "but what if someone doesn't have a gift?"

"Nonsense!" said Alice B. Smith with a giggle. "Everyone has some sort of gift or other. It's just a matter of finding it . . ." She turned to the other pupils. "Now, everyone, why don't we show Ottoline what we've been working on?"

In the school hall, Brian the Invisible Boy and his dog, Bodge, demonstrated their remarkable gift for plate spinning.

"Why don't you have a go?" said
Alice B. Smith.

Ottoline tried plate spinning . . .

. . . without much success.

"Never mind," said Alice B. Smith cheerfully.
"Solihull will find Mr. Munroe a bandage."

In the school gymnasium,
the Wright sisters,
Orvillise and Wilburta,
demonstrated their
amazing gift for aerial
flower arranging.

99

"Let's see what you can do,"
said Alice B. Smith.

Ottoline tried aerial flower arranging . . .

. . . but she
dropped the
flowers and her
shoe came off.

101

"Cheer up," said Alice B. Smith after they
had bandaged Mr. Munroe's hand. "Flower
arranging isn't everyone's cup of tea."

In the school dining room, the Sultana of Pahang demonstrated her extraordinary gift for curtain origami.

Ottoline tried curtain
origami . . . but it was
harder than it looked.

Alice B. Smith nodded encouragingly. "Top
marks for effort," she said. "By the way, you're
standing on Mr. Munroe's toe, dear."

104

Outside in the school grounds, Cecily
and Mumbles demonstrated their gift
for carriage croquet.

Ottoline and Mr. Munroe tried
carriage croquet . . .

106

"Good shot!" laughed Alice B. Smith.

"Beginner's luck," said Cecily, taking back her mallet and ball and giving Mr. Munroe a particularly hard stare. "Besides, dogs aren't allowed to play. It's the rules."

In the school art room, Newton Knight the Boy Genius was demonstrating his artistic gifts.

"Newton is the cleverest boy in the world," explained Alice B. Smith. "He finds that painting helps his brain relax."

Ottoline tried
painting . . .

. . . and Mr. Munroe helped with the
paint pots.

"Oops!"
said Ottoline.
"Well, that's
certainly
different . . ."
said Alice B.
Smith.

# Chapter Eight

After lunch, everyone went home with their parents for Saturday night and Sunday morning. Everyone except for Ottoline and Cecily.

CAPTAIN WRIGHT →

← D KN

Ottoline's parents were away on a collecting trip and Cecily's parents were too busy.

THE INVISIBLE MAN

THE SULTAN OF PAHANG

112 "Of course, it's Mumbles I feel sorry for,"
Cecily said to Ottoline as they walked through
the modern-sculpture garden that afternoon.
"He misses my parents terribly. I wish school
was over and I could take him home."

That night, when Ottoline heard Cecily crying, she got out of bed and tiptoed over to her five-poster bed.

THE PICNIC CLUB
IN THE WOODS
*Admit* one + a friend
FROM MIDNIGHT TILL LATE
BLACK TIE

"What is it?" said Cecily, drying her eyes.

"I've got a plan," said Ottoline and she showed Cecily the invitation the bear had packed into her trunk. "It says to bring a friend."

THE CLOTHES
THE BEAR
PACKED

As they sneaked down the extremely grand staircase, Cecily told Ottoline all about the time her mother, Cecily Forbes-Lawrence II, had been a pupil at the Alice B. Smith school and had discovered a secret tunnel.

"Where?" asked Ottoline as they quietly opened the big front door and tiptoed out.

"If I told you," said Cecily, "then it wouldn't be a secret."

Ottoline and Cecily arrived at the Picnic Club and showed their invitation.

117

The bears certainly knew how to throw a
party. Ottoline and Cecily danced the Grizzly
Hokey Cokey and the Bear-Foot
Stomp . . .

They had tea for two, with
twin pots of Canadian
honey . . .

And then danced some more . . . until it was
quite late in the night or very early in
the morning. Ottoline
wasn't sure
which.

Then it began to
rain, and the bears packed
away their picnic and switched
off the lights. The party was over.

By the time Ottoline and Cecily got back to school it was a wild and stormy night. Lightning flashed overhead and thunder cracked.

They silently tiptoed up the extremely grand staircase. From behind them came a *Thump! Thump! Thump!*

"You don't think," said Ottoline, "that it could be the Horse of the Hammersteins, do you?"

"Of course not," said Cecily. But Ottoline could feel her friend trembling as she gripped her hand tightly. "It can't be . . ."

Slowly they both turned around and . . .

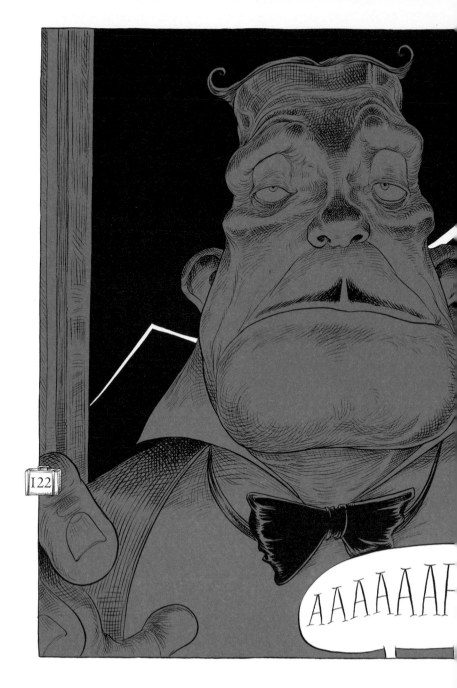

"I'm sorry I startled you," said Solihull the butler. "Let me hang up those wet jumpers and bring you some hot milk."

"You're not going to tell Miss Smith?" asked Cecily.

"Of course not, Miss Forbes-Lawrence," said Solihull. "

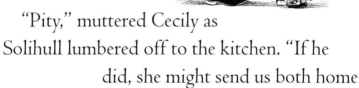

"Pity," muttered Cecily as Solihull lumbered off to the kitchen. "If he did, she might send us both home as punishment."

"But I don't want to go home," said Ottoline, hurrying up the stairs. "After all, I still haven't discovered what my different gift is."

# Chapter Nine

BY CAMEL CARAVAN

Professor & Professor
Brown,
c/o The Roving Collectors'
Society

Dear Ma & Pa,

Hope you are well. Bad news. I still haven't discovered what my different gift is. Mr. Munroe says my painting is interesting, but I don't believe him and the big pot of blue paint I was using has disappeared. Newton Knight the Boy Genius has lost his skateboard, and the Sultana of Pahang's pencil case is missing. As soon as I discover my gift I shall investigate,

lots of love,

X X X.

P.S. Solihull told me the weedkiller is missing from the garden shed!

P.P.S. Cecily got a letter from her parents' secretaries, saying her parents will write when they're not so busy!

COUNT HAMMERSTEIN & SON

127

THE QUESTING MAID

PING PONG

PAN MACMILLAN

CLIP
CLOP
CLIP
CLOP
CLIP

CLIP
CLOP
CLIP
CLOP

CLIP
CLOP

CLIP
CLOP

CLIP
CL

The scream came from Cecily. "Look!"
she said, pointing to the portrait of her
grandmother Cecily Forbes-Lawrence I.

"It's the curse of the Horse of the
Hammersteins!" she said dramatically.

"Oh dear," said Alice B. Smith, who had been woken by Cecily's scream and had come to find out what all the commotion was about. "What can it mean?"

133

"This school is HAUNTED!" said Cecily theatrically. "I think you should send us all home, Miss Smith."

"Such a wonderful imagination, Cecily dear."
Alice B. Smith smiled. "Let's all go back to
bed. Things will look better in the morning."

"I doubt it," said Cecily. "By the way, why
isn't Ottoline's dog in the East Wing?"

Everybody turned and looked at Mr.
Munroe. He was holding a red crayon in
his hand, and at his feet was the Sultana of
Pahang's missing pencil case. He had found
it on the floor outside the Forbes-Lawrence
Room just a moment ago.

"Bad dog!" said Cecily with a smile.

"I'm very disappointed in you, Ottoline," said Alice B. Smith. "Your pet's behaviour is your responsibility. Come and see me in my study tomorrow morning at thirteen o'clock sharp."

CANADIAN ARCTIC SOCKS THAT THE BEAR PACKED

135

# Chapter Ten

The next morning at thirteen o'clock, Ottoline and Mr. Munroe went to Alice B. Smith's study.

"As punishment for scribbling on Cecily Forbes-Lawrence I," said Alice B. Smith, "I want you to write out, 'I must supervise my pet more closely'."

"Yes, Miss Smith," said Ottoline. "How many times?"

"Just once," said Alice B. Smith, giving Ottoline a large sheet of paper, "but in very big letters."

Ottoline and Mr. Munroe were in the art room writing out their line in big letters when Mr. Munroe thought he heard something over by the door.

"Stay where you are," said Ottoline, drawing an extra big "SELY". "I've got to supervise you more closely. We'll finish this and then go and investigate together."

A moment later Brian and
Bodge walked in . . .

ART ROOM

139

140

"It's the curse of the Horse of the Hammersteins," said Cecily, who just happened to be passing by. "We should all leave now!"

So that's where my blue paint went, thought Ottoline.

"Shouldn't you take your line to Miss Smith?" said Cecily helpfully.

Ottoline and Mr. Munroe exchanged looks . . .

They set off for Alice B. Smith's study and were passing the staircase when Mr. Munroe saw something on the second to top step.

"We'll give this line to Miss Smith and then go and investigate together," said Ottoline.

141

EMERGENCY!
EMERGENCY!

142

Just then
Newton and
Skittles appeared at
the top of the stairs . . .

"MY SKATEBOARD!"
said Newton.

"It's the curse of the Horse of the
Hammersteins," said Cecily, who just
happened to be passing by. "No one is safe!"
Ottoline and Mr. Munroe exchanged looks.

They reached Alice B. Smith's study and Ottoline was about to knock on the door when they both heard a *snip-snipping* sound coming from the school dining room.

Mr. Munroe looked at Ottoline.

"We should investigate now," said Ottoline.

"It's the curse," said Cecily, who just happened to be passing by, "of—"

"The Horse of the Hammersteins. I know, I know," said Ottoline.

"It'll only get worse!" warned Cecily.

Just as Mr. Munroe spotted the pruning shears lying on the floor behind a chair leg, two loud screams echoed down the corridor.

Ottoline and Mr. Munroe began to run in the direction of the school gymnasium.

"It's the Horse of the Hammersteins!" Cecily called after them.

Mr. Munroe held up the empty bottle of weedkiller he had spotted in the corner of the gymnasium.

"I think the Horse of the Hammersteins has gone too far this time," said Ottoline. "Don't you?"

Mr. Munroe nodded. "What on earth is all this commotion about?" asked Alice B. Smith.

"We're frightened," said Alice B. Smith's Differently Gifted pupils. "We think the school is haunted!"

Alice B. Smith laughed a tinkling little laugh. "Oh," she said, "the ghosts here at the Alice B. Smith School are all very friendly." She smiled. "I wouldn't let them stay if they weren't. You leave the matter with me. I'm sure there won't be any more trouble."

"Well, if there is," said Cecily firmly, "we shall tell our parents to come and take us home!"

All the Differently Gifted pupils nodded except for Ottoline.

Alice B. Smith gave everyone the rest of the day off to think things over. "You can decide tomorrow morning," she said, "after a good night's sleep."

"I don't suppose the ghost will let us get a good night's sleep, do you?" said Ottoline to Cecily.

149

# The day passed slowly . . .

OTTOLINE LIKED TO BRUSH MR. MUNROE'S HAIR WHEN SHE WAS THINKING UP CLEVER PLANS

CECILY LIKED TO BRUSH MUMBLE'S MANE BEFORE CARRIAGE-CROQUET PRACTICE

OTTOLINE'S NOTE BOOK

CLEVER PLAN.

M.M.

150

. . . until at last it
was bedtime. 151

Everybody climbed into Cecily's five-poster
bed.

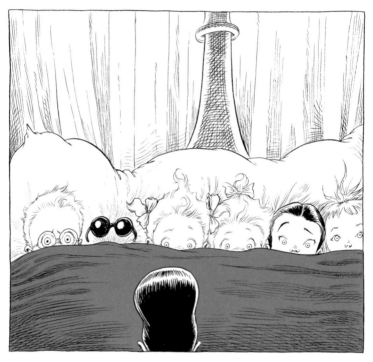

"If we don't leave the Alice B. Smith
School for the Differently Gifted tomorrow,"
said Cecily with a smile, "then we'll all be
DOOMED!"

 "We'll see about that," said Ottoline.

153

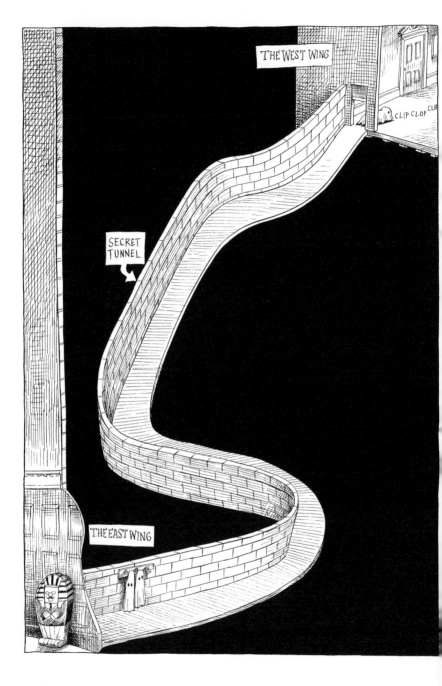

CLIP

CLOP

CLIP

CLOP!

"I can hear something!" whispered Newton.

"So can I," said Brian.

"I'm frightened," said Orvillise.

"Me too!" said Wilburta.

"The ghost is coming!" trembled the Sultana of Pahang.

"I told you so," said Cecily. "Didn't I, Ottoline . . . ? Ottoline? Ottoline . . . ?"

GIRLS' DORMITORY

BOYS' DORMITORY

157

Suddenly some bright lights came on . . .

. . . a beautifully
woven floral net
dropped . . .

. . . and the
ghost was
bundled up
in an expertly
folded parcel.

159

Leave now before
it is too LATE!

"It's all right, there's no need to be frightened," said Ottoline to the Alice B. Smith Differently Gifted pupils. "Show them, Mr. Munroe."

Mr. Munroe stepped forward.

He unwrapped the parcel, snipped through the beautifully woven floral net and pulled off the white sheet . . .

WOOF!

162

"Mumbles!" exclaimed Alice B. Smith,
who'd come to see what all the commotion
was about.

The next morning, Alice B. Smith called a special assembly.

"Congratulations, Ottoline," she said. "You've discovered your gift!"

"I have?" asked Ottoline.

"Yes," said Alice B. Smith, pinning a shiny badge to Ottoline's blazer.

ALICE B. SMITH
SCHOOL

DIFFERENT GIFTS

NEWTON KNIGHT - ROBOT PAINTING

THE SULTANA OF PAHANG - CURTAIN ORIGAMI

BRIAN INVISIBLE - PLATE SPINNING

ORVILLISE & WILBURTA WRIGHT - AERIAL FLOWER ARRANGING

CECILY FORBES-LAWRENCE - CARRIAGE QUET

OTTOL BROWN

THIS IS OTTOLINE'S BADGE

ALICE B. SMITH SCHOOL
SPOOK SPOTTING
DIFFERENT GIFT

MR. MUNROE WAS GIVEN A BADGE TOO

164

Ottoline looked at the badge.

"I couldn't have done it without a clever plan," she said, "and a little help from my friends."

Then, glancing at Cecily, who was looking very sorry and ashamed of herself, she leaned forward and whispered into Alice B. Smith's ear.

Alice B. Smith listened and nodded slowly. "You're right," she said, patting Ottoline on the shoulder. "You really are Differently Gifted, my dear."

Professor & Professor Brown,
C/o The Roving Collectors'
Society

Dear Ma & Pa,
The school isn't haunted
by the Horse of the Hammersteins. It was
just one of Cecily's stories. She was homesick
but is very sorry for causing a fuss.
Alice B. Smith is sending her home early
with a school report. I'm looking forward
to showing you mine!

lots of love,

× × ×.

P.S. I found my different
gift! Mr. Munroe helped me.
He sends his love.

166

# ALICE B. SMITH SCHOOL

# REPORT

NAME: MR. & MRS. FORBES-lauRENCE II

| SUBJECT | GRADE | COMMENTS |
|---|---|---|
| BEDTIME STORIES | B- | you both TELL VERy good STORiES WHEN you're not too BUSy! |
| QUALITY TIME | D | not ENOUGH tiME SPENt with CECiLy - MUST do BetteR. |
| HOLIDAYS | F | you MUST take MORE holidays with CECiLy - VERy disappointing. |
| FUN AND GAMES | F | not ENOUGH of either bECAUSE you're BOtH too BUSy. MUST botH try haRdER. |
| PERSONAL DEVELOPMENT | C- | CECiLy thiNKS you BOtH haVE potENtial but ONLy if you chaNGE youR attitudE. |

GENERAL COMMENTS:

VERy disappointing But CECiLy and I thiNK that you CAN BotH IMPROVE as paRENts if you apply yOURSELVES. WE hopE you'll do bEttER in fUTURE.

aLiCE B. SMitH

ALICE B. SMITH   HEADMISTRESS

The next day a large fancy car rolled up the drive and Mr. and Mrs. Forbes-Lawrence got out. Solihull showed them to Alice B. Smith's study.

When they came out Mr. Forbes-Lawrence was very red in the face and Mrs. Forbes-Lawrence had tears in her eyes. They both gave Cecily a big hug.

"Enjoy an extra long holiday together," said Alice B. Smith, waving goodbye. "And we'll see you next term, Cecily."

"Goodbye, Cecily," said Ottoline. "See you in the holidays."

"By the Turtle Pool," said Cecily with a smile, "in Pettigrew Park and Ornamental Gardens."

Mr. Munroe gave Mumbles an iced bun he'd saved especially.

"I like Cecily," said Ottoline. "She is my second-to-best friend."

Mr. Munroe didn't say anything. He just squeezed Ottoline's hand.

ALICE B. SMITH SCHOOL

HAIRY
HELPFULNESS

A    S

DIFFERENT GIFT

THIS IS
MR. MUNROE'S
BADGE

First published 2008 by Macmillan Children's Books
a division of Macmillan Publishers Limited
20 New Wharf Road, London N1 9RR
Basingstoke and Oxford
Associated companies throughout the world
www.panmacmillan.com

ISBN 978-1-4050-5058-6

Text and illustrations copyright © Chris Riddell 2008
All rights reserved.
Printed and bound in China

7986

# ALICE B. SMITH'S SPOOK GUIDE

**HEADLESS HUMPHREY** ENJOYS A REALLY GOOD BOOK AND SLIDING DOWN THE BANNISTERS

**MOLLY COBWEB** EXPLORES SPIDERY CORNERS AND DUSTY DRAPES

**THE HAPPY HOUSEMAID** DUSTS BEHIND THE PRANCING UNICORN

**ACCRINGTON STANLEY** IS IN LOVE WITH THE QUESTING MUSE

**THE DANCING DUKE** DOES A GHOSTLY JIG TO THE MUSIC OF A THREADBARE MINSTREL

**THE WHITE KNIGHT** WEARS A DIFFERENT SUIT OF ARMOUR EVERY NIGHT

**THE SEA CAPTAIN** LOVES POMERANIAN PICKLES

**THE GIGGLING DUCHESS** MIRROR MIRROR ON THE WALL, SHE'S THE GIGGLIEST OF THEM ALL!

The ghosts at the Alice B. Smith School
are very friendly.
Did you spot them all?

CHAIR MONITOR

WEEPING WORKSHOP

GIGGLING STUDIES

ADVANCED MUSING

TEA SIPPING

BEING

BURP CLUB

CONKERS TEAM

LOOKING

SEEMING

PAPER FOLDER

WHISTLING CHOIR